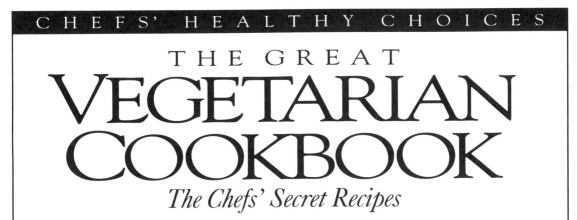

THE GREAT
VEGETARIAN
COOKBOOK

The Chefs' Secret Recipes

By Kathleen DeVanna Fish

Library of Congress Cataloging-in-Publication Data

THE GREAT VEGETARIAN COOKBOOK
The Chefs' Secret Recipes

First printing, 1994

Fish, Kathleen DeVanna
93-070483
ISBN 0-9620472-1-X
$14.95 softcover
Includes indexes
Autobiography page

Editorial direction by Fred Hernandez
Cover photography by Robert N. Fish
Cover design by Morris Design
Food styling by Susan Devaty
Illustrations by Robin Brickman
Chef portraits by Elna Mira Bjorge – Ultimate Productions
Type by Cimarron Design

Published by Bon Vivant Press
a division of The Marketing Arm
P.O. Box 1994
Monterey, CA 93942

Printed in the United States of America
by Publishers Press

Contents

Great Recipes
from Great Chefs

he *Great Vegetarian Cookbook* offers an unbeatable combination: four-star chefs and food that's healthful as well as delicious.

This innovative book is geared to a new era of cuisine. It will appeal to non-vegetarians who would like an occasional change from meats. And it will appeal to dedicated vegetarians as a source of innovative, imaginative and easy-to-prepare recipes.

Here's how *The Great Vegetarian Cookbook* works. We selected 43 of America's best chefs, including many superstars of the culinary world. We asked them to share their best meatless recipes. These are seldom revealed secrets — recipes geared toward better ways of eating. The chefs have lowered the oil, butter and sugar contents of dishes with novel techniques that don't sacrifice taste and traditional flavors.

The Great Vegetarian Cookbook offers 180 kitchen-tested recipes from chefs who give meatless dining a gourmet appeal. The emphasis is on fresh foods, high fiber and low fat. As you will see, this is not necessarily a diet book. This is a book about healthy, hearty and delicious food. The recipes are listed according to courses: Starters, Soups, Salads and Dressings, Breads, Rice, Pasta and Grains, Main Courses, Side Dishes, Sauces and Condiments, and Final Temptations.

The recipes have been adapted for the home cook, using contemporary ingredients in an easy-to-use format that includes preparation and cooking times. Some of the recipes are simple. Some are more complex. We stayed clear of purely trendy foods, preferring to stress foods that we know are wonderful.

You will discover a wide range of styles and specialties: dishes with roots in France, Mexico, Italy, the Caribbean, Asia, California, the Southwest and the Middle East. This cookbook traverses a wide range of culinary and ethnic food traditions, resulting in a fabulous collection of creative, simple and clean dishes.

But we wanted to bring you more than just listing ingredients and oven times. We wanted you to get to know these incredible chefs, to hear what they had to say about cooking, about ingredients, about methods and what they like to eat when they dine out. We wanted you to know what ingredients they can't live without, and to see how the chefs look.

In a section we call Listen to the Chefs, our guest chefs suggest many good, quick meals. Some talk about how they got interested in cooking. They talk about the things that many cooks do wrong. They provide fascinating insights into their own cuisines.

There is a revolution in the way we think about food. It is no longer enough that the end result tastes good. We now recognize the link between diet and good health, and healthy food preparation has become a challenge to all chefs — in the home and in the four-star kitchen. That is why *The Great Vegetarian Cookbook* goes one step further. We include a directory of mail-order food outlets so that anybody, anywhere, can get ingredients which may not be available locally. You will also find a glossary of ingredients as well as a measurement conversion guide. Finally, we offer a special guide to selecting wines which complement vegetarian dishes.

No doubt, some people will continue to scoff at the new cuisines of healthful dishes. Here's how to handle them: Prepare a meal from this book, such as Spicy Sweet Potato Bisque, Stuffed Chiles with Wild Mushrooms in a Saffron Sauce, Garlic Roasted Mashed Potatoes and Blood Orange Soufflé, then invite them over for dinner. It's as simple as that.

☆

Chefs' Favorite Recipes

Starters

Soups

Salads and Dressings

Breads

Rice, Pasta & Grains

Main Courses

Side Dishes

Sauces & Condiments

Final Temptations

America's Cooking Stars

ACQUERELLO

SUZETTE GRESHAM-TOGNETTI

1722 Sacramento Street
San Francisco, CA 94109
415-567-5432

ITALIAN CUISINE

ARCADIA

ANNE ROSENZWEIG

21 East 62nd Street
Manhattan, NY 10021
212-223-2900

AMERICAN CUISINE

BAYONA

SUSAN SPICER

430 Rue Dauphine, French Quarter
New Orleans, LA 70112
504-525-4455

MEDITERRANEAN CUISINE

BORDER GRILL

SUSAN FENIGER AND MARY SUE MILLIKEN

1445 4th Street
Santa Monica, CA 90401
310-451-1655

MEXICAN/CENTRAL AMERICAN CUISINE

BRASSERIE LE COZE

ROBERT HOLLEY

2901 Florida Avenue
Coconut Grove, FL 33133
305-444-9697

FRENCH CUISINE

CAFÉ BEAUJOLAIS

MARGARET FOX

961 Ukiah Street
Mendocino, CA 95460
707-937-5614

CALIFORNIA CUISINE

CENTRAL 159

DAVID BECKWITH

15th Street
Between Lighthouse Avenue and Central Avenue
Pacific Grove, CA 93950
408-655-4280

CALIFORNIA CUISINE

CHEF ALLEN'S

ALLEN SUSSER

19088 N.E. 29th Avenue
Aventura, FL 33180
305-935-2900

SOUTH FLORIDA CUISINE

CHEZ PANISSE

ALICE WATERS

1517 Shattuck Avenue
Berkeley, CA 94709
510-548-5525

MEDITERRANEAN CUISINE

DALI

MARIO LEON-IRIARTE

415 Washington Street
Somerville, MA 02143
617-661-3254

SPANISH CUISINE

DEUX CHEMINÉES

FRITZ BLANK

1221 Locust Street
Philadelphia, PA 19107
215-790-0200

FRENCH CUISINE

DRAGO

CELESTINO DRAGO

2628 Wilshire Boulevard
Santa Monica, CA 90403
310-828-1585

ITALIAN CUISINE

EMERIL'S

EMERIL LAGASSE

800 Tchoupitoulas Street
New Orleans, LA 70130
504-528-9393

GULF COAST CUISINE

THE FOUR SEASONS

HITSCH ALBIN

99 East 52nd Street
New York, NY 10022
212-754-9494

CONTINENTAL/AMERICAN CUISINE

GALILEO

ROBERTO DONNA

1110 21st Street N.W.
Washington, D.C. 20036
202-293-7191

ITALIAN CUISINE

GERONIMO

GINA ZILUCA

724 Canyon Road
Santa Fe, NM 87501
505-982-1500

SOUTHWEST CUISINE

THE GRANGE HALL

KEVIN JOHNSON

50 Commerce Street
Manhattan NY 10014
212-924-5246

AMERICAN CUISINE

GREENS

ANNIE SOMERVILLE

Fort Mason, Building A
San Francisco, CA 94123
415-771-6222

VEGETARIAN CUISINE

THE HAY-ADAMS HOTEL

PATRICK CLARK

800 16th Street N.W.
Washington, D.C. 20006
202-638-6600

AMERICAN CUISINE

INN OF THE ANASAZI

PETER ZIMMER

113 Washington Avenue
Santa Fe, NM 87501
505-988-3236

SOUTHWEST CUISINE

KASPAR'S

KASPAR DONIER

2701 First Avenue
Seattle, WA 98121
206-441-4805

AMERICAN/FRENCH CUISINE

THE LARK CREEK INN

BRADLEY OGDEN

234 Magnolia Avenue
Larkspur, CA 94939
415-924-7766

AMERICAN CUISINE

L'ESPALIER

FRANK MCCLELLAND

30 Gloucester Street
Boston, MA 02115
617-262-3023

FRENCH CUISINE

LESPINASSE

GRAY KUNZ

St. Regis Hotel
2 East 55th Street
New York, NY 10022
212-339-6719

FRENCH CUISINE

THE MANSION ON TURTLE CREEK

DEAN FEARING

2821 Turtle Creek Boulevard
Dallas, TX 75219
214-559-2100

REGIONAL TEXAS CUISINE

MARK'S PLACE

MARK MILITELLO

2286 N.E. 123rd Street
North Miami, FL 33181
305-893-6888

REGIONAL FLORIDA CUISINE

MICHELA'S

JODY ADAMS

1 Athenaeum Street
Cambridge, MA 02142
617-225-2121

ITALIAN CUISINE

MIKE'S ON THE AVENUE

MIKE FENNELLY

628 St. Charles Avenue
New Orleans, LA 70130
504-523-1709

SOUTHWEST ASIAN CUISINE

OCCIDENTAL GRILL

TRENT CONRY

1475 Pennsylvania Avenue N.W.
Washington, DC 20004
202-783-1475

AMERICAN CUISINE

THE OCEAN GRAND

HUBERT DES MARAIS

2800 S. Ocean Boulevard
Palm Beach, FL 33480
407-582-2800

REGIONAL FLORIDA CUISINE

PATINA

JOACHIM SPLICHAL

5955 Melrose Avenue
Los Angeles, CA 90038
213-467-1108

FRENCH/CALIFORNIA CUISINE

THE PLACE AT YESTERDAY'S

ALEX DAGLIS

28 Washington Square
Newport, RI 02840
401-847-0125

ECLECTIC CUISINE

THE PRINCE & THE PAUPER

CHRIS BALCER

24 Elm Street
Woodstock, VT 05091
802-457-1818

CONTINENTAL/AMERICAN CUISINE

THE RITZ-CARLTON, BUCKHEAD

GUENTER SEEGER

3434 Peachtree Road, N.E.
Atlanta, GA 30326
404-237-2700

EUROPEAN/AMERICAN CUISINE

ROVER'S

THIERRY RAUTUREAU

2808 East Madison
Seattle, WA 98112
206-325-7442

FRENCH CUISINE

ROXSAND

ROXSAND SUAREZ

2594 East Camelback Road
Phoenix, AZ 85016
602-381-0444

FRENCH/AMERICAN CUISINE

SALEH AL LAGO

SALEH JOUDEH

6804 East Greenlake Way North
Seattle, WA 98115
206-524-4044

ITALIAN CUISINE

SQUARE ONE RESTAURANT
JOYCE GOLDSTEIN

190 Pacific Avenue
San Francisco, CA 94111
415-788-1110

MEDITERRANEAN CUISINE

TOPOLOBAMPO
RICK BAYLESS

445 N. Clark
Chicago, IL 60610
312-661-1434

REGIONAL MEXICAN CUISINE

VINCENT GUERITHAULT ON CAMELBACK
VINCENT GUERITHAULT

3930 East Camelback Road
Phoenix, AZ 85018
602-224-0225

SOUTHWEST CUISINE

ZEFIRO
CHRISTOPHER ISRAEL

500 N.W. 21st Avenue
Portland, OR 97209
503-226-3394

MEDITERRANEAN/PACIFIC COAST CUISINE

ZINFANDEL
RICK BAYLESS

59 West Grand
Chicago, IL 60610
312-527-1818

MEXICAN CUISINE

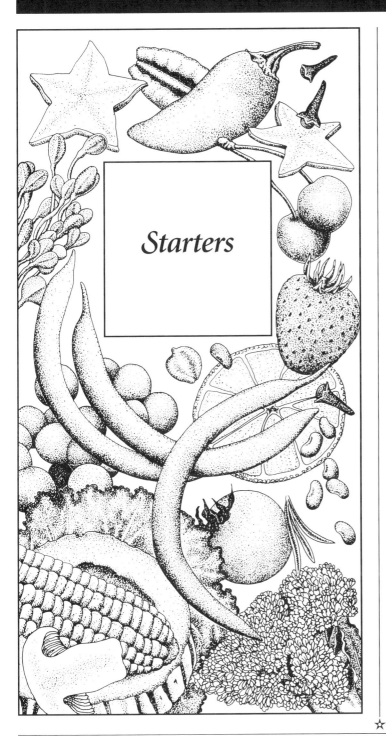

Starters

Goat Cheese Stuffed Artichokes with Riesling Wine

Bruschetta with Gorgonzola and Walnuts

Eggplant Caviar

Pan-Fried Goat Cheese and Roasted Bell Peppers

Goat Cheese Crouton with Mushrooms in Madeira Cream

American Corn Fritters

Potato Fritters with Yogurt & Chutney

Onions on Potatoes with Truffle Vinaigrette

Goat Cheese Spring Rolls

Sweet Garlic Capri Cheese Soufflé

Tapenade

Goat Cheese and Broccoli Wontons

Goat Cheese Stuffed Artichokes with Riesling Wine

Serves 4
Preparation Time:
  30 Minutes
Cooking Time:
  30 Minutes

  4 **medium artichokes**
    Juice of 1 lemon
  ¼ **cup olive oil**
  1 **red onion, peeled,**
    sliced
  1 **carrot, peeled, sliced**
  1 **cup Riesling wine**
  1 **bay leaf**
  1 **sprig of thyme**
2½ **garlic cloves, peeled,**
    crushed
    Salt and pepper to
    taste
  6 **oz. goat cheese**
  2 **Tbsps. black olives,**
    minced
  1 **tsp. parsley, chopped**
  1 **tsp. chives, chopped**
 20 **small cherry tomatoes**
    Olive oil

 ut off the stems and trim away all the outer leaves of the artichoke. Remove the choke filaments and trim the bottoms, removing all the green skin. Place trimmed chokes in a bowl of cold water with lemon juice.

Heat the olive oil in a saucepan. Add the onion and carrot and cook 3 to 4 minutes. Add the wine, followed by the artichokes, bay leaf, thyme, 2 cloves garlic, salt and pepper. Just cover with water and simmer 20 minutes. Remove the artichokes and set aside.

Combine the goat cheese, remaining garlic, olives, and salt and pepper to taste.

Fill each artichoke with the stuffing mixture. Place on a cookie sheet and warm through in the oven at 325°, about 10 minutes.

Bring the broth to a boil. Add parsley, chives and tomatoes. Season to taste.

Spoon the broth with tomatoes evenly divided into 4 shallow soup bowls. Place one artichoke in the center of each bowl. Drizzle with olive oil and serve. Garnish with additional basil if desired.

Patrick Clark
The Hay-Adams Hotel
Washington, D.C.

☆

Bruschetta with Gorgonzola and Walnuts

Sauté the garlic in olive oil. Remove from pan. Mix the gorgonzola and mascarpone cheese together until creamy. Add the walnuts.

Toast the bread on a grill. Rub the garlic on the toast, then drizzle with olive oil and spread the cheese.

Sprinkle parsley on top and serve.

Serves 4
Preparation Time:
  10 Minutes

- 1 garlic clove, chopped
- 2 tsps. olive oil
- 4 oz. gorgonzola cheese
- 4 oz. mascarpone cheese
- $\frac{1}{8}$ cup walnuts, finely chopped
- 4 slices of bread
  Parsley, chopped

Roberto Donna
Galileo
Washington, D.C.

Eggplant Caviar

Serves 4
Preparation Time:
  25 Minutes

  1 **large eggplant**
  ½ **small red onion,**
     chopped
  ¼ **tsp. garlic, minced**
  ½ **tomato, peeled, seeded**
  2 **Tbsps. olive oil**
     Salt and pepper to
     taste
     Juice of ½ lemon
  2 **Tbsps. parsley,**
     chopped
     Fresh basil, chopped,
     optional

rick the eggplant several times with a fork. In a broiler, or on a flat griddle or grill, roast the eggplant until the skin begins to blacken, the juices turn syrupy and the pulp feels completely soft.

Cool until touchable. Peel the eggplant and roughly chop the pulp.

Place the eggplant in a bowl and add the onion, garlic and tomato. Stir until smooth. Add the olive oil, salt, pepper and lemon juice to taste. Garnish with herbs.

Trade Secret: Serve with Susan Spicer's Tapenade on page 36 in separate dishes with toasted French bread or garlic croutons.

Susan Spicer
Bayona
New Orleans, Louisiana

Pan-Fried Goat Cheese with Roasted Bell Peppers

Slice cheese ½" thick.

Beat eggs in a mixing bowl. Place bread crumbs in a separate bowl.

Dip cheese slices in egg, then in bread crumbs. Set aside in a cool place.

Place all peppers a sheet pan. Brush with olive oil and place in the oven at 400°. Turn peppers often, until completely roasted, 12 to 15 minutes. Remove any charred skin, core and seeds.

Dice peppers and sauté in olive oil. Add the shallots, garlic and chives.

In a sauté pan, add 2 Tbsps. olive oil. When oil is hot, quickly sauté the cheese patties, 15 seconds per side.

To serve, drizzle the peppers with the sauce over the cheese patties.

Serves 4
Preparation Time:
  30 Minutes

  8 oz. goat cheese
  1 egg
  1 egg yolk
  ½ cup bread crumbs
  4 bell peppers
     (best if mixed colors)
  4 Tbsps. olive oil
  2 shallots, chopped
  1 garlic clove, chopped
  ½ bunch chives
     (optional)

Thierry Rautureau
Rover's
Seattle, Washington

Goat Cheese Crouton with Mushrooms in Madeira Cream

Serves 4
Preparation Time:
  20 Minutes

  4 oz. goat cheese,
    softened
  6 Tbsps. butter, softened
  4 slices whole-grain
    bread, toasted
  2 Tbsps. shallots, finely
    chopped
  ⅓ cup Madeira
  ¾ cup whipping cream
  ½ lb. mixed mushrooms
  ½ tsp. garlic
    Salt and pepper to
    taste
    Chives
    Parsley or celery leaves
    as garnish

ix the goat cheese and 3 Tbsps. butter. Spread on toasted bread. Trim the bread crusts and cut slices in half.

Simmer shallots in Madeira until liquid is reduced by half. Add cream, bring to a boil, reduce heat and simmer.

In a large pan, sauté mushrooms in 3 Tbsps. butter until golden. Toss in the garlic and the warm Madeira cream. Bring to a boil and cook for 2 to 3 minutes. Season with salt, pepper and chives to taste.

Place toast with cheese in a hot oven or broiler just long enough to brown a little. Remove from oven, arrange on plates and divide mushrooms among the four plates. Garnish with parsley or celery leaves.

Susan Spicer
Bayona
New Orleans, Louisiana

American Corn Fritters

ombine all dry ingredients in a medium mixing bowl.

In a separate bowl, combine the eggs and beer.

Quickly mix the wet ingredients into the dry, using as few strokes as possible. Add the corn. Add additional flour and cornmeal if necessary to desired thickness.

Heat oil to medium-high heat. Spoon in the fritters a few at a time. Cook about 3 minutes on all sides. Drain on a paper towel.

Serve with maple syrup.

Serves 4
Preparation Time:
  20 Minutes

½ cup all-purpose flour
1 Tbsp. sugar
¼ tsp. salt
2 tsps. baking powder
½ cup yellow cornmeal
2 eggs
½ cup non-alcoholic beer
2 ears corn, kernels
   scraped from the cob
   Oil for frying
   Maple syrup

David Beckwith
Central 159
Pacific Grove, California

☆

Potato Fritters with Yogurt

Serves 6
Preparation Time:
  45 Minutes

  2 Tbsps. mustard seeds
  1 Tbsp. whole cumin
     seeds
  2 Tbsps. clarified butter
  2 Tbsps. neem leaves,
     dried, crushed,
     optional
  1 onion, peeled, diced
  2 tsp. garlic, chopped
  ½ tsp. turmeric
  ½ bunch cilantro leaves,
     washed, roughly
     chopped
  1 serrano chile, seeded,
     stemmed, very finely
     diced
  ½ tsp. salt
  ¼ tsp. pepper
  2 lbs. potatoes, peeled
  1 cup Besan (chickpea)
     flour
  1 tsp. cumin
  ⅛ tsp. cayenne
  1 tsp. turmeric
  1 tsp. salt
  ½ tsp. pepper
  ½ cup water
     Oil for frying
     Plain yogurt

R oast the mustard seeds in a dry pan over medium heat until they become grayish, aromatic and pop. Add whole cumin seeds and roast until brown, being careful not to burn. Add the butter and neem leaves, browning lightly. Add the onions, garlic and turmeric.

Remove from heat and add the cilantro, serranos, salt and pepper. Set aside.

Cook the potatoes in salted water until soft. Drain, cool and grate. Gently mix the grated potatoes with the onions and spices. Season to taste. Form potato mixture into half-dollar size rounds.

To make the bhujia batter, combine the chickpea flour, cumin, cayenne, turmeric, salt and pepper and water. Mix until smooth and creamy.

Dip the potato rounds into the batter and drop into hot oil. Fry until golden brown on all sides. Drain well on a paper towel.

Serve warm on a platter with plain yogurt for dipping. The fritters can be made early in the day and reheated.

Susan Feniger &
Mary Sue Milliken
The Border Grill
Santa Monica, California

Baked Vidalia Onions on Potato Cakes with Truffle Vinaigrette

I n a saucepan, boil enough water to cover onions. Place whole, unpeeled onions in the water, return to a boil and cook 3 minutes.

Remove the onions and plunge them into ice water. When cold, peel by gently slipping off the skins.

Trim the root ends so that onions sit upright.

Cut two-thirds of the way through the top of the onions, dividing them into fourths or eighths. The onions should remain whole. Trim outer leaves to resemble a flower. Open the onions slightly by hand and place the butter or olive oil on top. Season with salt and pepper.

Place onions onto a greased baking dish or pan and bake at 500° for 5 to 7 minutes until sizzling hot and tips begin to turn brown.

Remove from oven and keep warm.

Peel and julienne baking potatoes to matchstick size. Do not wash, pat dry.

Place shortening into a large sauté pan or skillet on high heat.

Add the potatoes to the hot pan and arrange to resemble 4 pancakes about ½" thick. Pat them down with a spatula. Reduce heat to medium-high and cook until golden brown. Turn and brown the other sides. Remove and keep warm.

Prepare the vinaigrette by whisking together the vinegar, truffle juice and Madeira. Heat the mixture slowly, do not boil.

While still hot, vigorously whisk in the oil and finally stir in the truffles, chives, salt and pepper.

Serve the onion on the potato cake. Drizzle with the vinaigrette before serving.

Serves 4
Preparation TIme:
  30 Minutes

- 4 Vidalia onions
- 4 tsps. butter or olive oil
  Salt and pepper to taste
- 4 medium potatoes
- 1 cup shortening (or clarified butter or peanut oil)
- 2 Tbsps. white wine vinegar
- 1 Tbsp. truffle juice
- 1 Tbsp. Madeira wine, optional
- 4 Tbsps. oil
- 1 Tbsp. chives, chopped
- 1 Tbsp. black truffles, sliced (or canned truffle peelings)

Fritz Blank
Deux Cheminées
Philadelphia, Pennsylvania

✩

Goat Cheese Spring Rolls

Serves 4
Preparation Time:
  30 Minutes

1½ cups goat cheese
 ½ tsp. garlic, chopped
 ½ tsp. tarragon, fresh,
    chopped
  1 Tbsp. parsley, chopped
  1 green onion, thinly
    sliced
1½ tsps. Kalamata olives,
    chopped
  1 Tbsp. sun-dried
    tomatoes, chopped
1½ tsps. olive oil
 ½ tsp. black peppercorns,
    crushed
  1 egg, beaten
 10 spring roll wrappers
    Oil for deep-frying

ix all the ingredients together except the egg and wrappers.

Place a spoonful of the mixture on one corner of each spring roll wrapper. Fold in the sides and roll.

Brush the edges of each wrapper with the beaten egg to ensure it does not unroll.

Deep fry rolls until golden brown. Place on paper towel to absorb excess oil.

Trade Secret: Serve as an appetizer or accompaniment with a spinach salad or pasta.

Kaspar Donier
Kaspar's
Seattle, Washington

Garlic Capri Cheese Soufflé

Place garlic bulbs and olive oil in an oven-proof pot and cover. Place in the oven at 300° for 1½ hours until garlic is very soft. Remove garlic from the olive oil and cool.

Slice open tops of the garlic bulbs and pull out the center cloves, so that the remaining bulb is like a cup. Place the center sections of the garlic in a strainer and push through, resulting in a garlic paste.

In a heavy-bottomed pot over low heat add the garlic paste with 1 Tbsp. olive oil. Add the flour and cook for 5 minutes on medium heat.

Remove the pot from the heat and add the warm milk and capri cheese. Stir until smooth. Return to heat and simmer for 5 minutes. Add the herbs and remove from heat.

While the mixture is warm, stir in 5 lightly beaten egg yolks.

Whip the 5 egg whites into soft peaks and fold into the mixture.

Pour into the garlic cups. Bake at 400° for 15 minutes. Serve immediately.

Serves 6
Preparation Time:
  30 Minutes
Baking Time:
  1 Hour, 45 Minutes

12 **garlic bulbs**
 5 **cups + 1 Tbsp. olive oil**
½ **cup flour**
 1 **cup milk, warmed**
 9 **oz. capri cheese**
 1 **Tbsp. tarragon**
 1 **tsp. thyme**
 1 **Tbsp. chives, chopped**
 5 **eggs, separated**

Frank McClelland
L'Espalier
Boston, Massachusetts

✫

Tapenade

Serves 4
Preparation Time:
  5 Minutes

  ½ cup olives, pitted,
     rinsed
  1 Tbsp. capers, rinsed
  2 tsps. Dijon mustard
  2 Tbsps. water
  ¼ cup olive oil

 lace the first four ingredients in a blender or food processor and pulse until coarsely chopped. With the machine running, drizzle in the olive oil and purée until not quite smooth.

Trade Secret: Serve with Susan Spicer's Eggplant Caviar in separate dishes with toasted French bread or garlic croutons.

Susan Spicer
Bayona
New Orleans, Louisiana

Goat Cheese and Broccoli Wontons

Wrap one whole garlic bulb in foil. Separate and peel 20 cloves from remaining bulbs. Place cloves in a baking pan with olive oil and thyme. Roast all the garlic in the oven at 350° for 1 hour.

Cut flowerets off head of broccoli. Blanch flowerets in boiling water for 1 minute. Drain and dip immediately in ice water. Drain when cool.

Cut roasted whole garlic bulb in half and squeeze the garlic out into a bowl. Mash in the goat cheese and ½ cup Parmesan cheese. Generously grind pepper over mixture to taste. Fold in half of the broccoli flowerets.

Place a rounded tablespoon of the mixture onto a wonton wrapper. Wet the wrapper edges and place another wrapper on top. Seal the edges. Continue until mixture is all used.

Place wontons in rapidly boiling water for 3 minutes.

In a large sauté pan, melt butter over medium heat. Stir in garlic cloves, walnuts, vegetable stock, red pepper and remaining broccoli. Cook 1 minute. Drain wontons and add to mixture with remaining Parmesan cheese and salt and pepper to taste.

Serve hot with additional grated Parmesan cheese.

Trade Secret: Wontons can be prepared one day in advance and kept uncooked and covered in the refrigerator.

Serves 8
Preparation Time:
  30 Minutes
Cooking Time:
  1 Hour

- 3 garlic bulbs
  Olive oil
  Thyme sprigs
- 1 head broccoli
- ½ cup goat cheese, crumbled
- ¾ cup Parmesan cheese, grated
  Salt and pepper to taste
- 1 package wonton wrappers
- ¼ cup (½ stick) sweet butter
- 1 cup walnut pieces, lightly toasted
- ½ cup vegetable stock
- 2 sweet red peppers, roasted, peeled, diced

Anne Rosenzweig
Arcadia
New York, New York

✩

Soups

Cold Almond & Cucumber Soup

In a blender or food processor, blend almonds, garlic and salt with a little vegetable stock until almonds turn milky. Add the cucumber, then slowly the oil and then the vinegar. Finally, add the rest of the vegetable stock.

Serve very cold and garnish with grapes.

Trade Secret: This delicious and easy to prepare cold soup is from Andalucia, in the south of Spain.

Serves 6
Preparation Time:
   20 Minutes

   ¾ **cup blanched almonds**
   3 **garlic cloves, peeled**
   1 **tsp. salt**
   4 **cups vegetable stock**
   ½ **cucumber, peeled, seeded**
   4 **Tbsps. sherry or wine vinegar**
   5 **Tbsps. olive oil**
   18 **red or green seedless grapes**

Mario Leon-Iriarte
Dali
Somerville, Massachusetts

Asparagus and Sorrel Vichyssoise

Serves 4
Preparation Time:
45 Minutes

1 lb. asparagus
2 leeks
1 medium potato
2 Tbsps. clarified butter
2 Tbsps. flour
4 cups vegetable stock
1 cup heavy cream
Salt and pepper to
taste
¼ cup sorrel leaves,
chopped
Chives, chopped,
optional

Discard white ends of asparagus and chop the remaining stalks.

Trim the leeks, saving the white bottoms. Wash leeks thoroughly and chop.

Peel potato and cut into 1" cubes.

In a heavy saucepan, heat the clarified butter over medium heat. Add the leeks and asparagus and gently sauté for 10 minutes until lightly browned. Reduce the heat and add flour. Cook 5 minutes more, stirring occasionally. Add the stock and bring to a boil. Add potato and simmer about 15 minutes. Add the cream and simmer another 5 minutes. Remove soup from heat. Salt and pepper to taste.

Add the sorrel leaves to soup and purée in a blender. Remove and strain through a sieve.

Serve warm or chilled. Garnish with chopped chives if desired.

Chris Balcer
The Prince and The Pauper
Woodstock, Vermont

Black Bean Soup with Goat Cheese

Soak beans overnight in water.

In a large stock pot, combine the beans with water, vegetable stock, onion, whole peeled carrot, bay leaf and serrano chile. Bring to a boil, then simmer about 45 minutes. Remove the carrot and bay leaf.

Blend the remaining ingredients in a food processor on low. When blended, return the soup to the pot.

Add cream and bring to a boil. Salt and pepper to taste.

Ladle into individual soup bowls. Serve hot with a slice of goat cheese on top.

Serves 6
Preparation Time:
  20 Minutes
Cooking Time:
  45 Minutes
(note soaking time)

- 1 lb. black beans
- 1 qt. water
- 1 qt. vegetable stock
- 1 yellow onion, chopped
- 1 carrot, peeled
- 1 whole bay leaf
- 1 serrano chile pepper
- 1 cup heavy cream
  Salt and pepper to taste
- 6 slices mild goat cheese

Vincent Guerithault
Vincent Guerithault on Camelback
Phoenix, Arizona

✭

Bread and Tomato Soup

Serves: 6
Preparation Time:
  30 Minutes

  2 **lbs. tomatoes, chopped**
  ⅓ **cup olive oil**
  6 **garlic cloves**
    Salt & pepper to taste
  6 **cups vegetable stock**
  12 **basil leaves, chopped**
  6 **slices bread, dry, cubed**

ash and drain tomatoes.
    In a large stock pot, sauté the garlic in olive oil until golden brown, then remove.

Add the tomatoes to the pot and cook for 10 minutes. Salt and pepper to taste.

Add stock and chopped basil leaves and heat to a low boil.

Remove from heat. Add the bread and allow to steep for a few minutes.

Trade Secret: Pour into individual soup bowls and drizzle with olive oil. This hearty soup is delicious served hot or cold.

Roberto Donna
Galileo
Washington, D.C.

☆

Butternut Squash & Leek Soup with Gruyere Cheese & Thyme

Melt the butter in a thick-bottomed soup pot. Add the leeks, garlic, salt and thyme. Cook the leeks until tender. Add the wine and cook until the wine has reduced.

Peel, seed and cut the squash into small cubes, approximately 4 cups. Add the cubed squash to the soup and cover with the stock. Cook over medium heat until the squash takes on a rather smooth consistency. Thin the soup with more stock if necessary to desired consistency. Season to taste with salt and pepper. Sprinkle with grated Gruyere cheese and chopped fresh thyme.

Serves 6
Preparation Time:
  1 Hour

  2 **Tbsps. butter**
    White of 2 medium
    leeks, sliced
  4 **garlic cloves, minced**
    Salt to taste
  ½ **tsp. dried thyme**
  ½ **cup white wine**
  2 **medium butternut**
    squashes or any winter
    squash
    Black or white pepper
  5 **cups vegetable stock**
  ¼ **lb. Gruyere cheese,**
    grated
  1 **small bunch fresh**
    thyme, chopped

Annie Somerville
Greens
San Francisco, California

43

Chanterelle Cappuccino Soup

Serves 6
Preparation Time:
1 Hour

1½ lbs. chanterelle or
    morel mushrooms,
    heads sliced, stems
    chopped
1 onion, chopped
1 stalk celery, chopped
1 leek, chopped
3 shallots, minced
4 garlic cloves, crushed
2 qts. water
    Zest of one lemon
1 clove, whole
2 peppercorns
1 sprig parsley
1 tsp. thyme, dried
1 tsp. tarragon
2 bay leaves
2 cups white wine
2 tsps. olive oil
½ cup Madeira
⅓ cup heavy cream
    Salt and pepper to
    taste
    Lemon juice to taste
    Steamed milk
2 egg yolks, optional
    Herbs for garnish

lace mushroom stems, onion, celery, leek, 1 shallot, and half the garlic in a large stock pot. Add water and all herbs and spices. Bring to a boil and simmer for 10 minutes. Add 1 cup wine and continue to simmer another 15 minutes. Strain. Place the liquid back into the stock pot and continue to cook until reduced by half. Reserve.

Pour 1 tsp. olive oil in a skillet with the remaining shallots, garlic and sliced mushroom heads. Cook for 4 minutes, stirring constantly. Add the Madeira and 1 cup wine and let cook for 2 minutes.

Place the mushroom mixture in a blender with the vegetable bouillon and blend. Pour back into the stock pot and add the cream. Season to taste with salt, pepper and lemon juice.

To serve, top each bowl of soup with steamed milk from a cappuccino milk steamer or scald one cup of milk, allow to cool, then add 2 egg yolks and whisk in a double boiler until it foams.

Ladle on to the soup. Garnish with tarragon, parsley and/or chervil.

Frank McClelland
L'Espalier
Boston, Massachusetts

Curried Corn Chowder

n a large pan, sauté the onions in peanut oil until translucent.

Dilute the curry paste in water and add to the onions. Add the garlic, scallions, ginger, salt and pepper. Sauté until mixture is well cooked and aromatic. Add the corn and potatoes and stir. Add the stock and the cream.

Simmer for 45 minutes to 1 hour. Pour into a food processor or blender and purée. Season to taste.

Serves 6
Preparation Time:
  15 Minutes
Cooking Time:
  1 Hour

2 onions, finely diced
  Peanut oil for sautéing
2 Tbsps. red curry paste
1 cup water
3 Tbsps. garlic, chopped
3 scallions, chopped
3 Tbsps. ginger, ground
  Salt & pepper to taste
2 cups corn kernels,
  fresh or frozen
2 cups potatoes, finely
  diced
3 cups vegetable stock
2 cups heavy cream

Roxsand Suarez
Roxsand
Phoenix, Arizona

Smoked Corn and Grilled Sweet Potato Chowder

Serves 8
Preparation Time:
30 Minutes
Cooking Time:
30 Minutes

10 ears yellow corn
2 red onions, diced
10 Roma tomatoes, diced
2 poblano chiles, diced
2 sweet potatoes, sliced
2 Tbsps. olive oil
½ cup wild rice, cooked
2 qts. vegetable stock
4 garlic cloves, minced
1 Tbsp. thyme, chopped
2 chipotle chiles, minced
Juice of 3 limes
Salt and pepper to taste

oss corn, onions, tomatoes, poblanos and sweet potatoes with olive oil.

Set up grill with wet smoking chips. Arrange vegetables on grill and cover for 15 to 20 minutes. Make sure the grill is not too hot.

Cut corn off the cob and dice sweet potato slices. Combine smoked vegetables with all remaining ingredients in a large stock pot, bring to a boil and simmer for 10 minutes. Season to taste.

Trade Secret: For a nice addition to this soup, float Peter Zimmer's cilantro squash dumplings, page 153.

Peter Zimmer
Inn of the Anasazi
Santa Fe, New Mexico

Wild Mushroom Soup in Black Sesame Crust

Clean mushrooms and chop coarsely.

Heat olive oil in medium saucepan over medium heat. Add onion and mushrooms and sauté for approximately 3 minutes or until mushroom liquid is evaporated. Sprinkle with flour and mix well. Add vegetable stock and heavy cream and bring to a boil. Season with salt, pepper, nutmeg and thyme. Reduce heat to low and simmer for about 45 minutes.

Pour mixture into 8 oven-proof soup cups and cool to room temperature.

Unfold puff pastry sheets. Measure diameter of soup cups. Cut out 8 circles 1" larger than diameter of soup cups.

Evenly brush top of pastry circles with beaten egg. Lift one pastry circle and drape it over a soup cup with egg side down. Press border of pastry to sides of cup. Repeat process with remaining pastry circles.

Evenly brush top of pastries with egg and sprinkle with black sesame seeds.

Place cups in refrigerator and chill for at least 30 minutes.

Transfer cups to cookie sheet and bake at 350° for about 15 minutes or until golden brown.

Serves 8
Preparation Time:
  40 Minutes
Cooking Time:
  1 Hour

½ lb. morel mushrooms
½ lb. oyster mushrooms
½ lb. button mushrooms
1 Tbsp. olive oil
¾ cup chopped onion
3 Tbsps. flour
4 cups vegetable stock
2 cups heavy cream
1 tsp. salt
⅛ tsp. black pepper
⅛ tsp. nutmeg
1 sprig thyme, chopped, optional
1 package puff pastry sheets
1 egg, beaten
1 Tbsp. black sesame seeds

Kaspar Donier
Kaspar's
Seattle, Washington

Winter Wild Mushroom Soup

Serves 8
Preparation Time:
  15 Minutes
Cooking Time:
  30 Minutes

  2 **carrots, peeled, diced**
  2 **celery stalks, washed,**
    diced
  1 **medium red bell**
    pepper, diced
  1 **medium green bell**
    pepper, diced
  2 **leeks, washed, tops**
    cut, diced
  2 **Tbsps. butter, unsalted**
  1 **red onion, peeled &**
    diced
  2 **cups dry white wine or**
    1 cup sherry
  8 **cups vegetable stock**
  ½ **lb. shiitake**
    mushrooms, coarsely
    chopped
  1 **lb. button mushrooms,**
    coarsely chopped
  2 **chanterelles (optional),**
    coarsely chopped
    Salt and pepper to
    taste

I n a medium stock pot, sauté all the vegetables except the mushrooms in butter until tender, about 5 minutes. Add the wine and simmer for 10 minutes. Add the vegetable stock and simmer another 20 minutes. Add the mushrooms and remove from heat. Season to taste.

This soup can be made up to 5 days in advance.

David Beckwith
Central 159
Pacific Grove, California

☆

Roasted Pepper and Potato Soup

In a large soup pot, heat the olive oil. Sauté the onions and peppers with cumin, oregano, salt and bay leaf, stirring constantly until onions are translucent. Add the potatoes, tomatoes, water, wine, lime juice and tortillas. Let simmer until potatoes are soft.

Purée soup in a food processor until smooth.

Reheat to serve. Garnish with sour cream and a lime wedge.

Serves 8
Preparation Time:
  1 Hour

  4 Tbsps. olive oil
1½ yellow onions, peeled, diced
  5 red bell peppers, roasted, peeled
  3 yellow bell peppers, roasted
  1 Tbsp. cumin, ground
  1 Tbsp. oregano, dried
1½ Tbsps. Kosher salt
  1 bay leaf
  2 large baking potatoes, peeled, diced
  3 sweet potatoes, peeled, diced
  2 cups tomatoes, diced
 12 cups water
2½ cups white wine
    Juice of 5 limes
  6 corn tortillas, cut into pieces
    Sour cream
    Lime wedges

Gina Ziluca
Geronimo
Santa Fe, New Mexico

Pimiento Soup with Fried Polenta

Serves 8
Preparation Time:
  1 Hour
(note refrigeration time)

  4 cups water
  ¼ tsp. salt
  1 cup coarse cornmeal
  2 lbs. pimientos
  3 Tbsps. unsalted butter
  2 yellow onions, diced
  4 cups vegetable broth
  3 cups oil
    (peanut or vegetable)
    Salt and pepper to
    taste
    Balsamic vinegar

I n a pot, bring 3 cups water to a rolling boil over high heat, add the salt and whisk in the cornmeal, little by little. Reduce the heat and stir so that the polenta does not stick. Cook for another 4 minutes, stirring often, until the consistency is stiff and somewhat dry. Immediately transfer the polenta to a 10″×8″ oiled baking dish. Let the polenta stand for 5 minutes, then cover the dish and refrigerate for 1 hour or until very firm.

Grill the pimientos whole, until their skins blister and char very slightly. Transfer to a plastic bag or a container with a tight-fitting lid and let steam for 20 minutes. Remove the pimientos and peel away the charred skin. Do not rinse under water. Cut the pimientos in half and remove the seeds and stems.

Melt the butter in a 6 qt. pot and cook the onions 10 minutes. Add the pimientos and the water and stew together for 10 minutes, uncovered. Add the stock, bring to a boil and reduce the heat. Simmer for 20 minutes.

Remove the polenta from the refrigerator. Invert the baking dish onto a cutting board and cut the polenta into short sticks, approximately ½″ wide and 2″ long. Heat oil in a 10″ cast iron skillet and carefully add the polenta sticks to the hot oil to deep-fry them. Let the sticks brown evenly. When the polenta has turned a rich brown all over, remove it from the oil and let it drain on a towel-lined plate. Let cool slightly, then separate the sticks.

Transfer the soup in batches to a blender and puree for 2 minutes. Pass through a medium-fine sieve into another pot. Season to taste with salt, pepper and a little balsamic vinegar.

Serve the soup in warm bowls and garnish each bowl with several polenta sticks.

©"Chez Panisse Cooking"

Alice Waters
Chez Panisse
Berkeley, California

☆

Pumpkin Soup

In a large stock pot, lightly sauté the leeks in butter until limp but not browned.

Add the pumpkin, rice, brown sugar, ginger, tomato paste and water. Bring to a full boil over high heat; then adjust to a simmer, and cook for about 30 to 45 minutes or until the pumpkin is tender.

Transfer the soup to a food processor and purée.

Reheat the puréed soup and add the heavy cream. Season to taste with salt, pepper and mace. Before serving, garnish with nasturtium blossoms and/or toasted pine nuts.

Trade Secret: Serve soup in the scooped-out shells of small pumpkins.

Serves 6
Preparation Time:
 1 Hour

 1 cup leeks, sliced,
   whites only
 2 Tbsps. butter
 8 cups pumpkin, raw,
   cut into 1" cubes
 ⅓ cup rice, uncooked
 1 Tbsp. brown sugar
 2 tsps. ginger root,
   grated
 2 Tbsps. tomato paste
 2 to 3 qts. water, to cover
   pumpkin by 2"
 1 cup heavy cream
   Salt and pepper to
   taste
 ¼ tsp. mace, ground
   Nasturtium blossoms,
   optional
   Pine nuts, optional

Fritz Blank
Deux Cheminées
Philadelphia, Pennsylvania

Spinach and Mint Soup

Serves 4
Preparation Time:
  10 Minutes

  4 cups vegetable stock
  4 cups fresh spinach,
    cleaned
  6 tsps. fresh mint,
    chopped
    Lemon juice to taste
  1 cube tofu, cut into
    squares
  ½ cup cooked garbanzo
    beans
    Salt and pepper to
    taste
  4 lemon slices

Bring the vegetable stock to a boil. Reduce the heat slightly and add the spinach. Cook for about 30 seconds, then add the mint, lemon juice to taste, tofu and garbanzo beans. Season to taste with salt and pepper.

Pour soup into individual bowls and garnish with lemon slices.

©"The Morning Food Cookbook"

Margaret Fox
Cafe Beaujolais
Mendocino, California

Spicy Sweet Potato Bisque

L ightly sauté the onions and carrots for 5 minutes, add the sweet potatoes, thyme and stock. Let simmer until sweet potatoes are very soft. Add the jalapeño. Remove from heat and let partially cool.

Place soup in a blender in small amounts and purée while gradually adding cream. When all soup is puréed, add the maple syrup, lime juice, salt and pepper.

Garnish with chopped apple pieces.

Serves 4
Preparation Time:
 30 Minutes

- $1/2$ cup onion, chopped
- $1/2$ cup carrots, chopped
- 2 lbs. sweet potatoes, peeled, coarsely chopped
- $1/4$ tsp. thyme
- $1\frac{1}{2}$ cups vegetable stock
- 1 tsp. jalapeño pepper, chopped
- 2 cups heavy cream
- 2 Tbsps. maple syrup
- 2 Tbsps. lime juice
  Salt and pepper to taste
  Apple pieces, finely chopped as garnish

Alex Daglis
The Place at Yesterday's
Newport, Rhode Island

Tomato Basil Soup

Serves 4
Preparation Time:
  20 Minutes

  2 lbs. large tomatoes
     Salt and pepper to
     taste
  4 Roma tomatoes
 20 basil leaves, dried
     Olive oil to taste

ash, core and quarter the large tomatoes. Pass through a juice machine or food processor. Season soup with lemon juice, salt and pepper. Refrigerate.

Wash and core the Roma tomatoes. Blanch the tomatoes in hot water and remove the skins. Slice into circles. Place circles on a sheet pan. Season with salt and pepper. Sprinkle with olive oil and set aside to marinate.

Whisk the cold soup and ladle onto plates or into shallow bowls.

Place the basil leaves on the tomato slices and pile five high. Place tomato piles in the center of the shallow soup bowls. Drizzle with oil.

Guenter Seeger
The Ritz-Carlton, Buckhead
Atlanta, Georgia

Tomato Bisque

In a large pot, sauté onions in 6 Tbsps. butter along with dill seed, dill weed and oregano for 5 minutes or until onions are translucent. Add the tomatoes and vegetable stock.

Make a roux by blending 2 Tbsps. butter and 2 Tbsps. flour, whisking constantly over medium heat for 3 minutes without browning. Add roux to stock and whisk to blend. Add salt and pepper. Bring to a boil, stirring occasionally.

Reduce heat and simmer for 15 minutes. Add chopped parsley, honey, cream and half and half. Remove from heat and puree. Strain.

Serve warm with a dollop of sour cream.

Trade Secret: "This is the epitome of a comforting soup. It's creamy and rich and nourishing. Even though I am such a fan of fresh tomatoes, this is the one dish that I think may work even better with canned tomatoes."

©"Cafe Beaujolais"

Serves 4
Preparation Time:
  30 Minutes

½ cup chopped onions
½ cup unsalted butter
1 tsp. dill seed
1½ tsps. dill weed
1½ tsps. oregano
5 cups canned crushed
  whole tomatoes
4 cups vegetable stock
2 Tbsps. flour
2 tsps. salt
½ tsp. white pepper
¼ cup parsley, chopped
4 tsps. honey
1¼ cups heavy cream
⅔ cup half and half
  Sour cream

Margaret Fox
Cafe Beaujolais
Mendocino, California

Cold Tomato Cucumber Soup

Serves 8
Preparation Time:
  30 Minutes

  5 **cucumbers**
  1 **fennel bulb**
  2 **Tbsps. dill**
  2 **yellow bell peppers**
    Rice wine vinegar to
    taste
  5 **garlic cloves, 4 roasted**
    Salt and pepper to
    taste
 28 **Roma tomatoes**
 ¼ **cup basil, chopped**
    Tomato pulp for
    thickening

n a food processor or blender, coarsely process cucumbers, fennel, dill, peppers, vinegar, 1 unroasted garlic clove, salt and pepper. Remove from food processor. Set aside.

Coarsely process tomatoes, the 4 roasted garlic cloves, basil and tomato pulp to desired thickness. Salt and pepper to taste.

Serve at room temperature by spooning the cucumber soup in one side of a bowl and the tomato soup in the other side.

Hubert Des Marais
The Ocean Grand
Palm Beach, Florida

☆

Vegetable Court Bouillon

Place vegetables and garlic in a large soup pot. Add the water and all the herbs and spices. Bring to a boil and simmer for 10 minutes. Add 1 cup wine. Continue to simmer another 15 minutes and strain. Place the strained liquid back in the pot and continue to cook until reduced by half.

Serves 6
Preparation Time:
  45 Minutes

- ½ lb. chanterelle or morel mushrooms, chopped
- 1 onion, chopped
- 1 stalk celery, chopped
- 1 leek, chopped
- 1 shallot, minced
- 2 garlic cloves, crushed
- 2 qts. water
  Zest of one lemon
- 1 clove, whole
- 2 peppercorns
- 1 sprig parsley
- 1 tsp. thyme, dried
- 1 tsp. tarragon
- 2 bay leaves
- 1 cup white wine

Frank McClelland
L'Espalier
Boston, Massachusetts

Vegetable Soup Stock

Yield:
 5 cups
Preparation Time:
 45 Minutes

Tops of 2 medium
leeks, chopped
1 carrot, peeled,
chopped
1 medium potato,
chopped
2 celery stalks, chopped
2 bay leaves
1 Tbsp. fresh marjoram
1 Tbsp. fresh oregano
1 Tbsp. fresh thyme
1 Tbsp. fresh parsley
4 garlic cloves
2 black peppercorns
Pinch of salt
5 cups cold water

Combine all ingredients in a large pot. Cover with cold water and cook over moderate heat until the stock begins to boil. Turn down the heat and simmer for 30 minutes. Strain stock and discard cooked vegetables.

Annie Somerville
Greens
San Francisco, California

Chilled Summer Vegetable Soup

Heat the oil in a large saucepan. Cook the onion over medium heat until soft, but not brown. Add the garlic, potatoes, eggplant, zucchini, pepper, tomatoes, herbs and stock.

Bring the soup to a boil. Reduce heat and gently simmer the soup until the vegetables are soft.

Transfer the soup to a food processor and lightly purée. Salt and pepper to taste. Chill soup thoroughly.

Before serving, stir in the vinegar to taste and top with grated cheese.

Trade Secret: Mark often ladles this soup around inverted molds of Quinoa Salad, page 75. Drizzle with olive oil.

Serves 8
Preparation Time:
 45 Minutes
(note refrigeration time)

- ¾ cup olive oil
- 1 sweet onion, peeled, diced
- 2 garlic cloves
- 2 large potatoes, peeled, diced
- 1 medium eggplant, diced
- 2 medium zucchini, diced
- 2 red bell pepper, seeded, diced
- 4 medium tomatoes, quartered
- 1 tsp. thyme
- 1 tsp. Italian parsley
- 1 tsp. basil
- 1 qt. vegetable stock
  Salt and pepper to taste
- 2 Tbsps. vinegar
  Parmesan cheese, grated

Mark Militello
Mark's Place
North Miami, Florida

Salads
&
Dressings

Couscous Salad

Prepare couscous according to package directions. When cooked, add the shallots, mint, herbs, peppers, tomatoes, olive oil and lemon juice. Season to taste. Serve hot or cold.

Serves 4
Preparation Time:
  30 Minutes

 1 **cup couscous**
2½ **Tbsps. shallots,**
    chopped
 2 **Tbsps. mint, chopped**
 2 **Tbsps. mixed herbs of**
    choice, chopped
 ½ **cup red bell peppers,**
    roasted, chopped
 ½ **cup tomatoes, diced**
 ¼ **cup olive oil**
 ¼ **cup lemon juice**
    Salt and cayenne
    pepper to taste

Gray Kunz
Lespinasse
New York, New York

Cucumber, Red Onion and Tomato Salad

Serves 6
Preparation Time:
   10 Minutes
(note refrigeration time)

  4 to 5 cucumbers
  1 medium red onion,
    peeled, halved, thinly
    sliced
  1 medium tomato,
    cored, seeded, diced
 ½ cup olive oil
  3 to 4 Tbsps. red wine
    vinegar
  1 tsp. sea salt
 ½ tsp. pepper

 lice the ends off the cucumbers. Peel and split them in half lengthwise. Slice into ¼″ slices and place in a bowl.

Add the remaining ingredients.

Toss and chill for 30 minutes before serving.

Susan Feniger &
Mary Sue Milliken
The Border Grill
Santa Monica, California

Yogurt Dressing

In a blender or food processor purée the pepper with the basil.

In a mixing bowl combine the red pepper purée with the yogurt.

Trade Secret: At Lespinasse, Chef Gray Kunz serves the yogurt dressing with a triple salad of marinated vegetables, couscous salad and vegetable piperade. He arranges all three in a triangle on the plate, with his yogurt dressing around the sides.

Serves 4
Preparation Time:
  5 Minutes

1 large red bell pepper
4 basil leaves, preferably
  opal basil
1 cup yogurt

Gray Kunz
Lespinasse
New York, New York

Fennel & Blood Orange Salad

Serves 4
Preparation Time:
  15 Minutes
(note marinating time)

  1 cup olive oil
  2 tsps. hot pepper flakes
  ¼ cup orange juice
  ¼ cup lemon juice
    Salt and pepper to
    taste
  2 small fennel bulbs
  4 Blood or Valencia
    oranges
  2 bunches arugula,
    washed and dried
 24 olives

o make the hot pepper vinaigrette, heat the olive oil until hot but not smoking. Add the hot pepper flakes and remove from heat. Let the oil infuse for 30 minutes. When cooled, whisk in the lemon and orange juices, salt and pepper.

Quarter the fennel bulbs, remove core and cut into julienne strips. Store in ice water.

Peel the oranges and cut into sections.

Toss the arugula lightly with the vinaigrette and divide among four plates. Arrange the fennel, oranges and olives on top of the fennel and lightly dress with more vinaigrette.

Christopher Israel
Zefiro
Portland, Oregon

Fruit Salad with Grapefruit Sorbet

Slice pineapple into 8 rings about ½" thick. Core and hollow. Dice the pineapple fruit. Peel the orange and section into 8 slices. Peel kiwi and slice into 16 slices. Peel, core and slice apples. Wash and hull strawberries, leaving whole. Peel and slice the bananas.

Mix all the fruit in large bowl adding the raspberries, 2 Tbsps. sugar, vermouth and lemon juice. Let marinate about 1 hour in refrigerator.

Arrange fruit in center of hollowed pineapple rings, garnish with mint sprigs.

For the sorbet, blend the grapefruit juice and 4 Tbsps. sugar in a ice cream machine, about 30 minutes.

Serve fruit with one scoop of sorbet.

Serves 8
Preparation Time:
  1 Hour
(note marinating time)

  1 pineapple
  1 orange
  4 kiwi fruit
  2 apples
  8 strawberries, large
  2 bananas
  1 pt. raspberries
  6 Tbsps. sugar
  2 Tbsps. vermouth
  1 Tbsp. lemon juice
  8 mint sprigs
  1 cup grapefruit juice

Vincent Guerithault
Vincent Guerithault on Camelback
Phoenix, Arizona

Garden Salad with Tomato-Herb Vinaigrette

Serves 6
Preparation Time:
  15 Minutes

  Mixed garden greens
1 **cup olive oil**
1 **Tbsp. lemon juice**
2 **tsps. sugar**
1 **tsp. salt**
1 **tomato, skinned,**
  seeded
4 **fresh basil leaves**
  (or 1 tsp. dried)
½ **tsp. white pepper**
2 **tsps. Dijon mustard,**
  optional

ash and dry greens.
Place the remaining ingredients in a blender and purée until smooth.
Pour vinaigrette over salad and serve.

Chris Balcer
The Prince and The Pauper
Woodstock, Vermont

Autumn Greens with Balsamic Vinaigrette and Pecans

In a mixing bowl make the vinaigrette by combining the sugar, Dijon mustard, balsamic vinegar, garlic, red pepper flakes and salt. Whisk in the olive oil and season to taste. Set aside.

Blanch the pecans in boiling water for 45 seconds. Remove from water and toss with the walnut oil, Kosher salt and cayenne.

Place a single layer of pecans on a sheet pan and sprinkle with sugar. Bake at 250° for 3 minutes.

Toss the greens with the vinaigrette and pecans before serving.

Serves 4
Preparation Time:
  15 Minutes
Cooking Time:
  40 Minutes

  1 Tbsp. sugar
  2 Tbsps. Dijon mustard
  $\frac{1}{2}$ cups balsamic vinegar
  $1\frac{1}{2}$ tsps. garlic, finely
    chopped
  1 tsp. red pepper flakes
  1 tsp. salt
  $2\frac{1}{2}$ cups olive oil
  3 cups pecan halves
  1 Tbsp. walnut oil
  $2\frac{1}{2}$ Tbsps. Kosher salt
  $\frac{1}{8}$ tsp. cayenne
  2 Tbsps. sugar
    Mixed baby greens
    (radicchio, endive,
    butter lettuce,
    watercress, mizuma,
    oakleaf, etc.)

Mike Fennelly
Mike's on the Avenue
New Orleans, Louisiana

☆

Warm Lentil Salad & Risotto Pancake

Serves 6
Preparation Time:
  30 Minutes

  2 cups green lentils
  2 tsps. salt
  1 bay leaf
  1 head radicchio
  1 head frisee lettuce
  2 heads mache
  ½ bunch chervil
  2 cups saffron risotto,
     cooked
  2 Tbsps. cornmeal
  ¼ tsp. pepper
3½ Tbsps. olive oil
  2 large shallots, diced
  1 small yellow bell
     pepper, diced
  2 Tbsps. sherry vinegar

ash the lentils under cold running water. In a medium saucepan cook them with 3 cups water, 1 tsp. salt and 1 bay leaf. Bring to a boil and simmer for 7 to 10 minutes until cooked firm to the bite.

Wash the salad lettuces and greens well. Towel dry.

Shape the risotto into 6 pancakes. Dust with cornmeal and season with salt and pepper. In a medium fry pan, fry the pancake in 2 Tbsps. olive oil until browned and crisp.

Warm 1 Tbsp. olive oil in a sauté pan. Add the shallots and cook for 1 minute until translucent. Add the yellow peppers and lentils. Toss with the sherry vinegar and ½ Tbsp. olive oil.

Separate onto 6 plates. Finish each with a warm pancake.

Allen Susser
Chef Allen's
Aventura, Florida

Pickled Chanterelle Mushrooms

Wash mushrooms in cold water and drain.
Put remaining ingredients in a stainless steel pot, bring to a boil and simmer for 5 minutes. Add mushrooms to the pot and bring to a rapid boil. Simmer over low heat for 2 minutes.

Remove from heat and cool.

Store in a glass jar in the refrigerator.

Trade Secret: Serve as an antipasto, a salad or a side dish.

Serves 8
Preparation Time:
  20 Minutes

1½ lbs. chanterelle or
    button mushrooms
  5 cups water
  2 cups white wine
    vinegar
  5 Tbsps. sugar
  3 Tbsps. salt
  1 onion, medium,
    quartered
  1 tsp. peppercorns
  1 clove, whole
  3 bay leaves
  3 Anaheim peppers
  8 garlic cloves
  1 sprig rosemary
  2 to 6 jalapeño peppers
    (optional)

Kaspar Donier
Kaspar's
Seattle, Washington

☆

Grilled Portobello Club Salad

Serves 4
Preparation Time:
  45 Minutes

4 large portobello
  mushrooms
¼ cup white wine
1 Tbsp. garlic, minced
1 tsp. olive oil
½ tsp. black pepper
½ tsp. salt
1 medium avocado
1 medium yellow
  tomato
3 oz. goat cheese
1 head frisee lettuce

ut the stems off the mushrooms and reserve. Combine the white wine, garlic, olive oil, pepper and salt. Marinate the mushroom caps in this mixture.

Grill the mushrooms for about 3 minutes until cooked through, preferably on a wood-burning grill.

Peel and carefully slice the avocado very thin. Slice the yellow tomato very thin. Carefully slice the goat cheese with a hot knife, as thin as possible.

Cut the grilled portobello mushrooms into thirds, lengthwise across the top. Stack the mushroom slices, tomatoes, avocados and goat cheese alternately, finishing with a mushroom top. Cut pile in half and serve on a bed of frisee lettuce.

Allen Susser
Chef Allen's
Aventura, Florida

Orange Salad with Olives

With a small sharp knife, peel the oranges, removing completely the white pith. Cut into thick slices.

Rinse the lettuce and cut into bite-size pieces. Place the lettuce, orange slices and onion in a serving dish.

Combine the oil, vinegar, salt & pepper together. Pour over the salad. Add the olives and toss well. Chill before serving.

Serves 4
Preparation Time:
20 Minutes

4 oranges
1 head Romaine lettuce
1 red onion, sliced thin
⅓ cup olive oil
1 Tbsp. sherry vinegar
¾ cup black olives, pitted
  Salt and pepper to
  taste

Mario Leon-Iriarte
Dali
Somerville, Massachusetts

☆

Hearts of Palm Ceviche

Serves 6
Preparation Time:
  20 Minutes
(note marinating time)

  ½ **fresh large heart of**
     palm
     Juice of 6 large limes
  1 **large serrano chile,**
     julienned
  1 **large red onion, shaved**
     thin
  2 **large tomatoes,**
     skinned, sliced
  1 **Tbsp. chives, snipped**
  1 **Tbsp. chervil leaves**
  2 **Tbsps. cilantro leaves**
     Salt to taste

Peel the bark from the hearts of palm, removing about half of its bulk until the flesh is soft and pliable. Slice the heart very thin on a short bias.

Marinate this in the fresh sqeezed lime juice for 1 hour.

Add the serrano chiles, red onion, tomato filets, chives, chervil and salt. Toss well and let marinate about 1 hour before serving.

Allen Susser
Chef Allen's
Aventura, Florida

☆

Orzo Pasta Salad

C ook pasta according to directions.
In a large mixing bowl toss the hot pasta with the other ingredients. Serve immediately.

Trade Secret: This makes an excellent main dish when served with fresh bread and cheese.

Serves 6
Preparation Time:
  15 Minutes

  1 lb. orzo (rice-shaped) pasta
  ½ cup sun-dried tomatoes (plumped in warm water)
  ½ cup olives, pitted, sliced
  ½ cup artichoke hearts, quartered
  1 small red onion, minced
  1 red bell pepper, roasted, chopped
  2 tsps. thyme leaves, chopped (or other fresh herbs)
    Juice of 2 lemons
  2 Tbsps. balsamic vinegar
  ½ cup olive oil
  1 Tbsp. Italian parsley, chopped
    Salt & pepper to taste

Susan Spicer
Bayona
New Orleans, Louisiana

Pear & Walnuts with Romaine Hearts, Watercress & Radicchio

Serves 6
Preparation Time:
   15 Minutes
Pre-heat oven to 375°

   3 Tbsps. sherry vinegar
   1 small shallot, minced
      Salt to taste
   4 Tbsps. light olive oil
   4 Tbsps. walnut oil
   ½ cup walnuts, chopped
   2 heads romaine lettuce
   1 small head radicchio
   2 bunches watercress
   2 ripe Comice pears,
      cored, sliced
      Freshly-ground black
      pepper

Prepare the walnut sherry vinaigrette by mixing together the vinegar, shallot and salt. Whisk in the oils to emulsify. Set aside.

Toast walnuts in a 375° oven for 10 minutes, until they begin to brown. Set aside to cool.

Rinse the greens and spin dry. Toss the salad greens, pears and walnuts with the walnut-sherry vinaigrette. Sprinkle with black pepper and serve.

Annie Somerville
Greens
San Francisco, California

☆

Quinoa Salad

Place the quinoa in a strainer and rinse thoroughly with cold water. Transfer to a saucepan and add the water. Bring to a boil, reduce the heat, and simmer for 10 minutes, or until all the water is absorbed and the grain is tender and separates easily. Let cool.

Combine all ingredients for the salad in a mixing bowl and toss. Allow salad to marinate for 1 hour. Add salt, pepper and lemon juice to taste.

Serves 6
Preparation Time:
 30 Minutes
Cooking Time:
 10 Minutes
(note refrigeration time)

 1 cup quinoa
 2 cups water
 1 cup cucumber, peeled, seeded, diced
 1/2 cup fennel, diced
 1 cup English peas, blanched
 1/2 cup celery, diced
 1 cup sweet corn kernels, blanched
 1/2 cup lemon juice
 2 Tbsps. olive oil
 1/3 cup mint, chopped
 1/2 cup basil, chopped
 Salt and pepper to taste

Mark Militello
Mark's Place
North Miami, Florida

☆

Roasted Pear and Radicchio Salad with Toasted Walnuts and Balsamic Vinaigrette

Serves 4
Preparation Time:
30 Minutes

2 pears, cut in half
1 head radicchio lettuce,
   quartered
   Olive oil
   Salt and pepper to
   taste
   Balsamic vinegar
4 oz. gorgonzola cheese
½ cup heavy cream,
   optional
1 bunch watercress,
   stems trimmed,
   washed, dried
1 shallot, peeled, sliced
   thin
½ cup toasted hazelnuts,
   chopped

Toss the pear halves and radicchio quarters in olive oil and season with salt and pepper. Place the pears and radicchio, sliced side down, in a roasting pan. Roast in the oven for 10 to 15 minutes at 450°.

Remove the radicchio from the oven, it should be crispy. Continue to cook the pears until they are tender and golden brown.

To serve, toss the warm pears and radicchio in a bowl with balsamic vinegar and olive oil. Arrange on four plates. Place a piece of gorgonzola on each plate. Just before serving, warm the plates in the oven for 4 minutes or until the cheese just begins to melt.

Toss the watercress and shallots in a bowl with balsamic vinegar, olive oil, salt and pepper. Place a mound of watercress in the center of each plate and garnish with hazelnuts.

Trade Secret: For a richer dish, reduce the cream by one fourth. Whisk in the gorgonzola until smooth. Salt and pepper to taste. Put a spoonful of gorgonzola sauce on a warm plate. Arrange the pear and radicchio on the plate.

Jody Adams
Michela's
Cambridge, Massachusetts

Fig Slaw

 n a food processor, puree the figs. Combine the fig purée with the lemon juice, zest, cabbage and pumpkin seeds.

Serves 4
Preparation Time:
   10 Minutes

   3 fresh figs
      Juice and zest of
      1 lemon
   1 cup cabbage, finely
      shredded
   ½ cup pumpkin seeds,
      toasted

Roxsand Suarez
Roxsand
Phoenix, Arizona

☆

Warm Spinach Salad with Grilled Onion, Ancho Chile and Pears

Serves 8
Preparation Time:
  15 Minutes

  1 cup walnut oil
  $\frac{1}{2}$ cup rice wine vinegar
  1 Tbsp. ginger, chopped
  3 ancho chiles, julienned
  3 red onions, grilled and
    sliced
  1 Tbsp. mustard seeds
  1 bunch cilantro
  3 Tbsps. mint, chopped
  $\frac{1}{2}$ cup honey
  1 lime, peeled, diced
  3 bunches spinach,
    cleaned
  $\frac{1}{4}$ cup apricots, fresh or
    dried, sliced
  4 red pears, sliced
  1 cup walnuts, roasted
    and chopped
  24 endive spears
  $\frac{1}{2}$ cup bleu cheese,
    crumbled (optional)

Prepare the dressing by combining together the oil, vinegar, ginger, chiles, onions, mustard seed, cilantro, mint, honey and lime. Pour the dressing into a small saucepan and bring to a boil. Remove from heat and set aside.

In large mixing bowl combine the spinach, apricots, pears and walnuts. Gently mix in the hot dressing and toss well.

Arrange 3 endive spears on each plate, place salad in middle and crumble cheese to garnish.

Trade Secret: Use Peter Zimmer's Potato Tumbleweeds, on page 166, as a garnish instead of cheese.

Peter Zimmer
Inn of the Anasazi
Santa Fe, New Mexico

Marinated Vegetables

Cut the spaghetti squash in half and scrape out the seeds. Place the squash skin side up in a large saucepan, cover by 2" with water, and bring to a boil. Lower the heat, cover, and simmer for 20 minutes.

While the spaghetti squash is cooking, steam or boil the beets in water until cooked and tender, about 30 minutes. Cool, then slice thin.

Using a fork, scoop out the center of the spaghetti squash; it will form spaghetti-like strands. Gently toss it with the sliced beets, mango, cucumber, lime zest, tarragon, ginger and corn oil. Season to taste with salt, pepper and sugar.

Bring the tarragon vinegar to a boil and pour over the salad to taste.

Trade Secret: At Lespinasse, Chef Gray Kunz serves the marinated vegetables in a triple salad with his couscous salad and vegetable piperade. He arranges all three in a triangle on the plate, with his yogurt dressing around the sides.

Serves 4
Preparation Time:
  45 Minutes

1 small spaghetti squash
4 beets
1 mango, sliced
½ small cucumber, sliced
1 Tbsp. lime zest
1 tsp. fresh tarragon, chopped
1 Tbsps. fresh ginger, minced
2 Tbsps. corn oil
  Salt, pepper and sugar to taste
  White tarragon vinegar to taste

Gray Kunz
Lespinasse
New York, New York

☆

Vegetable Piperade

Serves 4
Preparation Time:
  15 Minutes

  1 small eggplant,
    julienned
  ¼ cup onions, coarsely
    chopped
  ¼ cup tomatoes, coarsely
    chopped
  1 red pepper, julienned
  1 yellow pepper,
    julienned
  1 Tbsp. olive oil
    Salt and pepper to
    taste

 Sauté all the vegetables separately. Allow each to cool, then mix together.

Season with olive oil, salt and pepper before serving.

Gray Kunz
Lespinasse
New York, New York

⭐

Olive and Red Onion Vinaigrette

In a large mixing bowl combine all of the ingredients. Let stand 2 hours or more.

Trade Secret: This vinaigrette is delicious warm or cold served on your favorite pasta.

Serves 6
Preparation Time:
  15 Minutes
(note marinating time)

  2 cups olives, pitted & roughly chopped
  3 green bell peppers, roasted, peeled, seeded, julienned
  $\frac{1}{2}$ large red onion, very thinly sliced
  $\frac{1}{2}$ cup champagne vinegar
  1 Tbsp. garlic, chopped
  1 tsp. Kosher salt
  $\frac{1}{2}$ cup Italian parsley, roughly chopped
  $1\frac{1}{2}$ cups olive oil

Gina Ziluca
Geronimo
Santa Fe, New Mexico

Hot Pepper Vinaigrette

Serves 4
Preparation Time:
 5 Minutes
(note marinating time)

 1 cup olive oil
 2 tsps. hot pepper flakes
 ¼ cup orange juice
 ¼ cup lemon juice
    Salt and pepper to
    taste

eat olive oil until hot but not smoking. Add the hot pepper flakes and remove from heat. Let the oil infuse with the pepper flakes for 30 minutes. When cooled, whisk in lemon and orange juices, salt and pepper.

Christopher Israel
Zefiro
Portland, Oregon

✩

Breads

Cheese and Wine Bread

Yields: Two loaves
Preparation Time:
 40 Minutes
(note rising time)
Cooking Time:
 30 to 40 Minutes

 ½ **cup green onions,**
  minced
 6 **Tbsps. garlic, finely**
  minced, optional
 6 **Tbsps. unsalted butter**
 2 **packages dry yeast**
 4 **tsps. sugar**
 ¼ **cup warm water**
1½ **cups dry white wine**
 2 **eggs, beaten**
 1 **tsp. salt**
 6 **to 6½ cups flour**
 1 **lb. aged Asiago or dry**
  jack cheese, cut into
  ½**" cubes**

 auté onions and garlic in butter for about 30 seconds. Remove from heat and set aside to cool.

Dissolve yeast and sugar in water. Stir and set in warm place for 5 minutes. Mixture should be bubbly. Stir again.

In a large bowl, whisk together the wine, eggs, salt and yeast mixture. Gradually add 3 cups flour, and beat for about 3 minutes until elastic threads start to form around edge of bowl. Add cooled garlic and onion mixture. With a large sturdy wooden spoon, beat in 2½ to 3 cups more flour.

Turn dough out on a very lightly floured board, and knead until smooth and springy. Cover with a clean dry dish towel and let rest 5 minutes. Knead again. If dough is tacky, add ¼ cup more flour and knead 5 more minutes.

Place dough in a large greased bowl, turn so it is greased all over, and seal airtight with plastic wrap. Put in a warm place and let rise until doubled, about 1 hour. Punch down, turn out, and knead a few times to pop air bubbles.

Divide dough in half and knead half the cheese into each piece, forming 2 balls. Put in a warm place, cover with a dish towel and let rise until almost doubled, about 45 to 60 minutes. Grease two 9"×5" pans and shape each ball into logs long enough so that the dough touches the ends of the pan.

Bake at 375° for 25 minutes. Reverse pans (top to bottom, front to back) and bake for another 5 to 15 minutes. Check by tapping on the bottom of the pans. They should sound hollow when done. Remove loaves from pan and cool on wire racks for at least 30 minutes before slicing.

©"Cafe Beaujolais"

Margaret Fox
Cafe Beaujolais
Mendocino, California

Skillet Sun-Dried Tomato & Cheddar Bread

Combine all dry ingredients in a medium mixing bowl. Stir in jalapeño, cheddar and chopped tomato.

In a separate bowl, whisk together eggs and milk. Stir liquids into the dry mixture and then mix in the peanut oil.

Lightly oil and heat an 8" cast-iron skillet until very hot. Pour in batter and bake at 400° for approximately 40 minutes. If using an 8" baking pan, add an additional 20 minutes to the cooking time.

Trade Secret: "The basics of this recipe come from an old Iowa family cookbook to which I have tried to give a little twist of the kaleidoscope to update for a more modern taste."

Yield:
  8 to 10 servings
Preparation Time:
  20 Minutes
Cooking Time:
  40 Minutes

  2 cups yellow cornmeal
  2 cups all-purpose flour
  ¼ cup granulated sugar
  2 Tbsps. baking powder
  1 jalapeño, seeded,
    finely diced
  1 cup cheddar cheese,
    grated
  ½ cup sun-dried
    tomatoes, chopped,
    drained of oil
  2 eggs
  2 cups milk
  ⅔ cup peanut oil

David Beckwith
Central 159
Pacific Grove, California

Tuscan Bread

Yield:
　2 large loaves
Preparation Time:
　4 Hours
(note standing time)

1¼ tsps. active dry yeast
¼ cup warm water
3 cups water, room
　temperature
⅘ cup or 200 grams Biga
　(recipe follows)
4½ cups all-purpose flour
3 cups bread flour
4 tsps. salt

Biga
¼ tsp. active dry yeast
¼ cup warm water
¾ cup plus 1 Tbsp. water,
　room temperature
2½ cups all-purpose flour

Stir yeast into ¼ cup warm water, let stand until creamy. Add remaining water and Biga to the yeast mixture. Add flour and salt, mixing until the dough binds well. Knead dough well, making sure to use enough flour to prevent sticking. Place dough in a lightly oiled bowl, cover and let rise until tripled in bulk, about 3 hours. Do not punch down.

To shape loaves, use a generous amount of flour on work surface and hands to prevent sticking. Dust dough with flour and cut in half. Flatten dough out and tightly roll lengthwise into a log shape. Flatten out the log and roll tightly from top to bottom. Shape each piece into a ball by slowly stretching top layer from top to bottom (seamside). Place loaves on baking sheet covered with baking parchment paper, seamside down. Cover with a damp towel and let rise until doubled in bulk, about one hour.

Bake at 450° until a deep golden brown and hollow sounding when tapped on the bottom, about 40 minutes.

Biga
Stir yeast into ¼ cup warm water and let stand until creamy, about 10 minutes. Add remaining ingredients to yeast mixture and mix with a wooden spoon 3 to 4 minutes. The result will be a loose, sticky dough.

Place dough in a lightly oiled bowl, cover with plastic wrap and let stand at even room temperature for 2 days. Afterwards, keep refrigerated. The dough will keep for approximately 2 weeks. Bring to room temperature before using.

Trade Secret: I recommend using a clay baker or place a pan of hot water on oven bottom for first 15 minutes of baking.

Suzette Gresham-Tognetti
Acquerello
San Francisco

☆

Buckwheat Dill Muffins

Mix dry ingredients in a bowl. Add the fresh dill. In a separate bowl, mix the remaining ingredients. Carefully combine all ingredients, taking care not to overmix.

Butter muffin cups and fill ⅔ full. Bake at 375° until done, approximately 10 to 15 minutes.

Yield: 12 muffins
Preparation Time:
 20 Minutes

- 1 cup all-purpose flour
- 1 cup buckwheat flour
- 1 tsp. salt
- ½ tsp. baking soda
- 1½ Tbsps. baking powder
- 4 Tbsps. granulated sugar
- 4 Tbsps. fresh dill, chopped fine
- 2 eggs
- 1¼ cups buttermilk
- ½ cup sweet butter, melted

Bradley Ogden
Lark Creek Inn
Larkspur, California

Name That Muffin

Yield:
  18 muffins
Preparation Time:
  15 Minutes
Cooking Time:
  30 Minutes

  2 **cups unsifted white flour**
  ¾ **tsp. salt**
  ¾ **tsp. baking soda**
  ¼ **tsp. baking powder**
  2 **eggs**
  ¾ **cup brown sugar**
  ¾ **cup corn oil**
  ¾ **tsp. vanilla extract**
  1⅓ **cups prepared fruit or vegetables**
  1½ **tsps. cinnamon**
  1½ **tsps. ground ginger**
  ⅓ **cup poppy seeds**
  ¾ **cup walnuts, toasted, chopped**

Sift together the flour, salt, baking soda and baking powder. In a separate bowl, whip the eggs with the sugar and oil. Stir in the vanilla, whatever fruits or vegetables you are using, the spices, and the poppy seeds. Then add the flour mixture and the nuts. Do not overmix.

Spoon the batter into greased or papered muffin cups, filling each about ¾ full. Bake for 25 to 30 minutes or until golden brown.

Variations:
    Apple or pear: Core and shred them.
    Zucchini: Shred them unpeeled
    Oranges: Wash well, chop up (skin, pulp and juice) and process in the bowl of a food processor. Add ⅓ cup extra poppy seeds, 1 extra tsp. ginger and ½ tsp. cinnamon.
    Pumpkin: Steam fresh pumpkin and cut into small bits.
    Tomato: Cut them into small bits.

Trade Secret: The personality of this muffin changes, depending on the fruit or vegetable that is added to the batter. One interesting option is to divide the batter into several batches and add different fruits or vegetables to each batch.

Margaret Fox
Cafe Beaujolais
Mendocino, California

Rice, Pasta & Grains

Angel Hair Pasta with Olive & Red Onion Vinaigrette

Caesar Salad Pasta

Fantasia di Farfalle

Linguine al Buon Gusto

Linguine with Cherry Tomato Vinaigrette

Pasta with Crispy Artichokes and Pea Sprouts

Pasta with Broccoli, Chickpeas, Onions and Tomatoes

Penne Pasta with Sofrito Sauce

Hazelnut Polenta

Creamy Wild Mushroom Polenta, Tomato Coulis

Polenta with Raisins, Pinenuts, Pomegranates & Sage

Raviolis Stuffed with Mushrooms & Garlic Potatoes

Raviolis in Pinenuts & Golden Raisins

Rice Pot with Yogurt and Herbs

Zucchini Rigatoni

Risotto alla Zucca

Risotto with Butternut Squash, Greens and Tomatoes

Risotto Cakes with Wild Mushrooms

Risotto and Mushroom Fricassee

Risotto with Wild Mushrooms

Squash and Mushroom Risotto

Risotto Verde

Angel Hair Pasta
with Olive and Onion Vinaigrette

Serves 6
Preparation Time:
  15 Minutes
(note marinating time)

  2 cups olives, pitted,
    roughly chopped
  3 green bell peppers,
    roasted, peeled,
    seeded, julienned
  ½ large red onion, very
    thinly sliced
  ½ cup champagne
    vinegar
  1 Tbsp. garlic, chopped
  1 tsp. Kosher salt
  ½ cup Italian parsley,
    roughly chopped
  1¼ cups olive oil
  1 lb. angel hair pasta,
    cooked

Combine all the ingredients except the pasta. Allow the flavors to marinate for 2 or more hours.
  Toss with the cooked pasta and serve either warm or cold.

Gina Ziluca
Geronimo
Santa Fe, New Mexico

Caesar Salad Pasta

I n a large sauté pan, warm the olive oil and garlic over low heat for 2 minutes. Add the lettuce and sauté over low heat, turning often until partly wilted, about 3 minutes. Add half the bread crumbs, the lemon zest and ½ cup grated Parmesan. Stir for another minute. Add the drained pasta, the pepper and toss well.

Place in a large serving bowl and top with the remaining Parmesan cheese and bread crumbs.

Trade Secret: In Italy, simple pasta with field greens and garlic is very popular, but not typical in America. However, people usually love Caesar salad, and love it as a pasta, too. Halve or quarter this recipe for a great small meal.

©"Back to Square One"

Serves 4
Preparation Time:
  15 Minutes

- 1 **cup olive oil**
- ¼ **cup garlic, finely minced**
- 12 **cups romaine lettuce or escarole, cut into ½" strips**
- 2 **cups toasted bread crumbs**
- 4 **tsps. lemon zest, grated**
- ¾ **cup Parmesan cheese, grated**
- 2 **tsps. black pepper**
- 1 **lb. spaghetti, cooked, drained**

Joyce Goldstein
Square One Restaurant
San Francisco, California

Fantasia di Farfalle

Serves 4
Preparation Time:
  15 Minutes

⅓ cup olive oil
1½ cups tomatoes, diced
2 tsps. garlic, finely
  chopped
  Salt and pepper to
  taste
4 oz. Brie cheese, rind
  removed
1 Tbsp. Italian parsley,
  chopped
4 large basil leaves,
  chopped
½ Tbsp. pine nuts,
  toasted
12 oz. Farfalle (bowtie)
  pasta
  Grated Pecorino
  cheese, optional
  garnish

Warm olive oil in a large sauté pan and add the tomatoes, garlic, salt and pepper. Toss over low heat for two minutes. Add the Brie, parsley, basil and pine nuts. Remove from heat when cheese has melted.

Cook the pasta in boiling salted water until al dente. Drain well and toss with sauce. Serve immediately.

Saleh Joudeh
Saleh al Lago
Seattle, Washington

☆

Linguine al Buon Gusto

I n a large sauté pan heat the olive oil over medium heat. Add the garlic, parsley, olives, and tomatoes. When mixture is hot add half of the goat cheese. Remove from heat. Salt and pepper to taste.

Cook the pasta in salted water until al dente. Do not overcook. Drain and toss with sauce.

Before serving, add the remaining cheese over the top.

Serves 4
Preparation Time:
  10 Minutes

  $^1/_2$ **cup olive oil**
  1 **Tbsp. garlic, minced**
  1 **Tbsp. Italian parsley,**
     minced
  8 **to 12 black olives,**
     pitted, quartered
  4 **oz. sun-dried**
     tomatoes, softened
     and diced
  6 **oz. goat cheese**
     Salt and pepper to
     taste
  1 **lb. linguine**

Saleh Joudeh
Saleh al Lago
Seattle, Washington

Linguine with Cherry Tomato Vinaigrette

Serves 4
Preparation Time:
25 Minutes

5 cups cherry tomatoes, preferably Sweet 100
1 cup virgin olive oil
Red wine vinegar
Salt and pepper
1½ cups fresh bread crumbs
1 handful fresh basil leaves
1 lb. linguine

The quality of this simple pasta depends on the excellence of the tomatoes (Sweet 100 is a varietal name. They are very small and intensely sweet.)

Cut the tomatoes in half and marinate them in olive oil, red wine vinegar to taste, and salt and pepper. Toast the fresh bread crumbs in the oven until dry and lightly browned. Take them from the oven and toss with some olive oil while still warm.

Cook the pasta, and while it is boiling, put the tomatoes in a pan and warm them. Add the pasta to the pan, toss together with the tomatoes, and serve.

Garnish the dish with the bread crumbs and basil leaves cut into tiny ribbons.

Variations: Peel large ripe tomatoes and quarter them. Dress them with virgin olive oil, red wine vinegar, salt and pepper, minced garlic, and lots of dwarf basil leaves.

Cook fresh noodles and toss the hot pasta with the cold tomatoes.

Finely dice peeled and seeded tomatoes. Season with salt, pepper, vinegar and chopped parsley, basil and coriander.

Boil linguine, drain, toss in olive oil, then mix with the tomato mixture and chill.

©"Chez Panisse Pasta, Pizza and Calzone Cookbook"

Alice Waters
Chez Panisse Cafe & Restaurant
Berkeley, California

Pasta with Crispy Artichokes and Pea Sprouts

To make the sauce, bring the stock to a boil. Add the truffle butter and truffle oil. Season to taste with salt and pepper.

Quarter the artichoke hearts and sauté in olive oil until golden brown. Add the butter and cook until crispy. Drain and set aside on a dry cloth.

Season pea sprouts with salt and pepper then quickly sauté in olive oil until tender. Drain.

Place pasta into boiling water and cook until al dente. Drain. Blend sauce with pasta, add the pea sprouts and top with the artichokes.

Serves 4
Preparation Time:
  25 Minutes

$^{1}/_{2}$ **cup vegetable stock**
3 **oz. truffle butter**
1 **Tbsp. truffle oil**
  Salt and pepper to taste
1 **cup artichoke hearts**
1 **Tbsp. olive oil**
2 **Tbsps. butter**
1 **cup pea sprouts**
  Pappardelle pasta

Gray Kunz
Lespinasse
New York, New York

Pasta with Broccoli, Chickpeas, Onions and Tomatoes

Serves 4
Preparation Time:
 25 Minutes
(note soaking time)

- ½ cup dried or canned chickpeas (garbanzos), or white beans
- 5 Tbsps. olive oil
- 1 large head broccoli, trimmed into small florettes
- ½ lb. rigatoni or orecchiette ("little ear") pasta
- 1 small red onion, diced
- 2 Tbsps. garlic, finely minced
- 2 cups canned plum tomatoes, diced
  Salt and pepper to taste
  Grated pecorino cheese, optional

 Soak dried chickpeas in 2½ cups cold water and refrigerate overnight. Drain and rinse the chickpeas. Place chickpeas in a small saucepan and cover them with lightly salted water. Bring to a boil over medium heat, then reduce heat and simmer covered, until tender but not mushy, about 1 hour. Drain the chickpeas and transfer to a bowl. Coat with 1 Tbsp. olive oil. Set aside to cool. If you use canned chickpeas, drain and rinse them. They will not be as firm as dried ones.

Blanch the broccoli florettes in salted water and refresh in ice water.

Bring a large pot of salted water to a boil. Drop in the pasta and cook until al dente, about 12 minutes.

While the pasta is cooking, heat the remaining olive oil in a large sauté pan over medium heat. Add the onions and cook until tender. Add the chickpeas, garlic, tomatoes and broccoli and warm all. Season with salt and pepper, then toss with the drained pasta.

Sprinkle with grated pecorino cheese, if desired.

Trade Secrets: Spice this up with a pinch of red pepper flakes in with the sautéed onions or you may add some chopped sun-dried tomatoes to the final sauce. This is a southern Italian pasta and is fun to eat. The central dimple in the orecchiette pasta is a perfect trap for the chickpeas.

Joyce Goldstein
Square One Restaurant
San Francisco, California

Penne Pasta with Sofrito Sauce

auté onions, half the garlic, and peppers in olive oil. Add tomatoes and simmer until stewed. Thicken with tomato paste if needed. Add herbs and season to taste.

Cook pasta in salted, boiling water until al dente.

Sauté the remaining garlic in olive oil. Toss garlic and olive oil in with pasta.

Serve sauce on top of the pasta. Garnish with herbs.

Serves 4
Preparation Time:
  20 Minutes

2½ Tbsps. olive oil
  1 red onion, diced
  2 garlic cloves, minced
  2 red bell peppers, diced
  1 yellow bell pepper, diced
  5 tomatoes, small, diced
    Tomato paste (optional)
  ½ bunch cilantro, chopped
  ¼ bunch oregano, chopped
    Salt and pepper to taste
  2 lbs. penne pasta

Hubert Des Marais
The Ocean Grand
Palm Beach, Florida

☆

Hazelnut Polenta

Serves 4
Preparation Time:
  15 Minutes

  3 cups milk
  3 Tbsps. butter
  1 egg yolk, beaten
  1 tsp. marjoram
  ¼ cup ground hazelnuts
  1 cup polenta
     (stone-ground yellow
     cornmeal)

I n a large saucepan, combine the milk, butter, egg yolk, marjoram and hazelnuts. Heat just to a simmer. Slowly add the cornmeal in a thin steam, whisking constantly. Lower the heat and continue stirring with a wooden spoon until the mixture thickens and leaves the sides of the pan, about 10 minutes.

Serve warm.

Gray Kunz
Lespinasse
New York, New York

Creamy Wild Mushroom Polenta

Bring the water and stock to a rolling boil in a oven-proof pot. Add the rosemary sprig, 2 tsps. garlic and polenta, stirring with a wooden spoon continuously to ensure there are no lumps, for 5 to 10 minutes.

Cover pot and place in preheated 350° oven, baking for 45 minutes, stirring occasionally. Remove from oven and add half the butter. Hold in a double boiler to keep warm.

Melt the remaining half of the butter in a sauté pan. Add the mushrooms, sautéing in the butter for 2 minutes. Add remaining 2 tsps. garlic and season with salt and pepper to taste. Sauté for another 2 to 3 minutes or until mushrooms are soft. Add mushrooms to the polenta with the herbs and sour cream. Season to taste if necessary and serve immediately.

Trade Secret: This dish is enhanced with a tomato coulis sauce.

Serves 6
Preparation Time:
  One Hour

- 2 cups water
- 2 cups chicken stock
- 1 3" sprig of rosemary
- 4 tsps. garlic, minced
- 1 cup polenta (cornmeal)
- 8 Tbsps. butter (1 stick), unsalted
- ½ lb. wild mushrooms, cleaned, trimmed, and sliced ¼" thick
- 1 Tbsp. Kosher salt
- 1 tsp. ground white pepper
- 3 Tbsps. each parley, sage and marjoram, chopped
- 1 cup sour cream or mascarpone

Bradley Ogden
Lark Creek Inn
Larkspur, California

☆

Polenta with Raisins, Pinenuts, Pomegranates and Sage

Serves 4
Preparation Time:
  40 Minutes
Cooking Time:
  40 Minutes

- 6 cups water
  Salt and pepper to
  taste
- 1 cup cornmeal
- ¼ cup Parmesan cheese,
  grated
- 2 Tbsps. unsalted butter
  Olive oil
- ¼ cup shallots, minced
- 2 Tbsps. garlic, chopped
- 1 cup Marsala wine
- 2 cups vegetable stock
- 1 Tbsp. balsamic vinegar
- 8 sage leaves, chopped
- ¼ cup pomegranate
  seeds
- 2 Tbsps. pinenuts
- 2 Tbsps. raisins, steeped
  in water just to cover
- ¼ lb. spinach leaves,
  cleaned

Bring 4 cups water to a boil in a large saucepan. Add salt. Mix the cornmeal with the remaining water and add to the boiling water in a steady stream. Whisk constantly until the polenta comes to a boil. Cook, stirring occasionally, for 40 minutes or until mixture is smooth and shiny. Add the cheese and butter. Salt and pepper to taste. Keep warm.

Heat two large frying pans with ⅛" olive oil in each. Add 2 Tbsps. minced shallots and 1 Tbsp. garlic to one of the pans with more oil if necessary. Cook for 3 minutes. Deglaze the pan with the Marsala and reduce to a glaze. Add the stock and reduce by ⅔. Add the vinegar, sage and pomegranate seeds and season with salt and pepper. Keep warm.

Add the remaining shallots and garlic with the pinenuts to the second pan. Cook until the nuts are golden and the shallots are tender. Add the raisins and the spinach, salt and pepper, and cook until the spinach is just wilted.

Place a large spoonful of the polenta on the side of a plate. Arrange the spinach on top and drizzle with sauce.

Jody Adams
Michela's
Cambridge, Massachusetts

☆

Ravioli Stuffed with Mushrooms, Garlic and Potatoes

Peel the potato and cut into 6 pieces. Place in a small pot and cover with water. Add a pinch of salt and cook until tender. Drain and push through a ricer while still warm. Beat in the mascarpone cheese. Season with salt and pepper.

Blanch garlic in salted water and cook until tender. Drain, cool, peel and coarsely mash. Add to the potatoes.

Finely chop one shallot. Heat 4 Tbsps. butter and cook the chopped shallot until translucent. Add the chopped mushrooms and cook until the mushrooms have released all their juices and the juices have been reduced. The mushrooms should be dry. Season with salt and pepper. Mix the mushrooms with the potato mixture. Add the parsley and thyme. Allow to cool.

Slice the remaining shallots in ⅛" slices. Heat the remaining butter in a small pan. When the foam subsides, add the shallots and cook until crispy. Keep warm. Save the butter for ravioli sauce.

Beat 1 egg with 2 Tbsps. water for egg wash. Brush the edges of a pasta sheet with the egg wash. Place 2 Tbsps. of the mushroom mixture in the center of the pasta. Make a well in the mixture. Crack an egg into a teacup. Pour the yolk and half of the white into the well. Cover with a second pasta sheet and push out as much of the air as possible. Seal the edges well. Place on a flour-dusted tea cloth. Repeat with remaining pastas.

Bring 5 qts. of water to a boil. Season with salt. Slip the raviolis into the water. Cook, stirring gently several times, for 5 minutes. Scoop out with a slotted spoon, drain, and place one on each plate. Drizzle with truffle oil or browned butter. Arrange the crisped shallots on top of each ravioli. Sprinkle with Parmesan cheese and garnish the plate with parsley.

Serves 8
Preparation Time:
  1 Hour

  1 potato
    Salt and pepper to taste
  ¼ cup mascarpone cheese
  8 garlic cloves, unpeeled
  4 shallots
  ½ cup (1 stick) unsalted butter
  1 cup mixed wild mushrooms, finely chopped
  1 Tbsp. parsley, chopped
  1 tsp. thyme, chopped
  9 eggs
 16 pasta sheets, 4"×4", for ravioli
    Truffle oil or browned butter
  ¼ cup Parmesan cheese, grated
  8 sprigs parsley

Jody Adams
Michela's
Cambridge, Massachusetts

☆

Ravioli with Pine Nuts and Golden Raisins

Serves 4
Preparation Time:
  20 Minutes

  4 Tbsps. butter, softened
  2 Tbsps. olive oil
  2 garlic cloves, finely
    chopped
  4 small shallots, finely
    chopped
  4 Tbsps. fresh tomato,
    chopped
  2 sun-dried tomatoes,
    finely sliced
  2 Tbsps. pine nuts,
    toasted
  2 Tbsps. golden raisins
  6 fresh basil leaves, cut
    into fine strips
  2 cups vegetable stock
1¼ lbs. fresh ravioli
    Grated Parmesan
    cheese

n a medium sauté pan, melt the butter with oil. When hot, add the garlic and shallots. Cook on high heat for 2 minutes. Add the tomatoes, pine nuts, raisins and basil. Add half the stock and simmer until reduced by half. Add the remaining stock and let reduce another 4 to 5 minutes.

Keep sauce warm while cooking ravioli until al dente.

Pour sauce over the ravioli and sprinkle generously with Parmesan cheese.

David Beckwith
Central 159
Pacific Grove, California

☆

Rice Pot with Yogurt and Herbs

Wash rice in warm water until water runs clear. Soak 6 to 8 hours or overnight in cold water with 1 Tbsp. salt to cover. Or soak in lukewarm salted water for 30 to 45 minutes.

Heat a large heavy-bottomed skillet and add 2 Tbsps. olive oil and the onions. Cook over medium heat until the onions start to become clear, about 10 minutes. Add the garlic, 1 tsp. salt, pepper and paprika and continue cooking, stirring often until aromas are released. Add the spinach and cook 3 to 5 minutes stirring often, until the spinach is wilted and the pan is almost dry. Set aside until rice is ready.

Boil $2\frac{1}{2}$ qts. water with 1 Tbsp. salt, drain rice and add to boiling water. Return to a boil and cook 10 to 12 minutes stirring occasionally. Rice should be cooked mostly through, except in the very center. Strain and rinse rice with warm water, shake gently to remove excess water.

In a large soup pot with a tight-fitting lid, melt the butter with the remaining olive oil. Add 2 Tbsps. water and sprinkle cooked rice evenly onto the bottom of the pot, one spoonful at a time until $\frac{2}{3}$ of the rice has been used. Spread the spinach mixture over the rice and cover with the remaining rice, mounding slightly in the center. Use the handle of a wooden spoon to poke about 5 holes in the rice, all the way to the bottom of the pot, for steam to escape. Cover the pot with a thick cotton dish towel and put the lid on tightly. Cook over medium-low heat 35 to 40 minutes.

Fill the sink with cold water. Remove cover from rice and prepare a large, round platter. Place the pot in the sink for 30 seconds. Remove and dry the bottom of the pot. Invert pot on the platter. Rice cake should unmold itself in one piece and be golden brown.

Mix the chopped herbs with yogurt and serve on the side of each serving of rice.

Serves 6
Preparation Time:
  45 Minutes
(note soaking time)
Cooking Time:
  40 Minutes

- 3 cups basmati rice
- 2 Tbsps. + 1 tsp. sea salt
- 4 Tbsps. olive oil
- 1 large onion, peeled, finely diced
- 5 garlic cloves, peeled, crushed
- $\frac{1}{2}$ tsp. pepper
- 1 tsp. paprika
- $\frac{1}{2}$ lb. spinach, washed, stemmed, roughly chopped
- 2 Tbsps. butter
- 1 bunch fresh basil leaves, roughly chopped
- 1 bunch fresh mint leaves, roughly chopped
- 2 cups plain yogurt

Susan Feniger &
Mary Sue Milliken
The Border Grill
Santa Monica, California

Rigatoni with Mint and Zucchini

Serves 4
Preparation Time:
  20 Minutes

- 2 Tbsps. garlic, minced
- 2 tsps. oil or butter
- 1 lb. rigatoni pasta, cooked, drained
- 2 zucchini, medium, chopped
- 8 mint leaves, chopped
- ½ cup Romano cheese, grated
- ¼ cup Italian bread crumbs
- Salt & pepper to taste

In a sauté pan, brown the garlic in oil or butter until golden. Add the zucchini and cook until tender. Add mint, salt and pepper.

Stir into cooked pasta. Toss in bread crumbs and romano cheese.

Celestino Drago
Drago
Santa Monica, California

☆

Risotto alla Zucca

Cut squash and yams in half lengthwise. Remove seeds from squash. Bake both on a sheet pan at 350°, cut sides down, for about 15 minutes. Turn over and spread lightly with butter. Bake until soft and lightly caramelized, about 10 minutes more.

With a spoon, scoop pulp from the squash and yams, leaving the skins.

In a heavy pan, heat the olive oil and 2 Tbsps. butter. Add the onions, shallots and garlic. Heat over medium-low heat until translucent. Do not caramelize. Add the rice. Stir until well coated and glistening. Add the white wine. Slowly add the stock, allowing the rice to absorb the liquid in between additions. Stir continuously. Do not allow the rice to settle and scorch. Add the squash & yam pulps to the rice.

Finish with nutmeg, salt and pepper, remaining butter and Parmesan cheese. Allow to cook slightly to absorb flavors before serving.

Serves 4
Preparation Time:
  40 Minutes
Cooking Time:
  25 Minutes

- 1 small (½ lb.) butternut squash
- 2 medium (½ lb.) jewel yams
- 6 Tbsps. (¾ stick) butter
- 1 Tbsp. olive oil
- ¾ cup white onion, minced
- 2 Tbsps. shallots, minced
- 1 tsp. garlic
- 1¾ cups Arborio rice
- 1 cup white wine
- 3½ cups vegetable stock, hot
- ¼ tsp. nutmeg
- 1½ tsps. salt
- 1½ tsps. white pepper
- ¼ cup Parmesan cheese, grated

Suzette Gresham-Tognetti
Acquerello
San Francisco, California

☆

105

Risotto with Butternut Squash, Greens and Tomatoes

Serves 6
Preparation Time:
  1 Hour

- **6 Tbsps. (¾ stick) butter or olive oil**
- **2 cups diced yellow onion**
- **2 cups Arborio rice**
- **2 cups butternut squash, cut into ½″ cubes**
- **6 cups vegetable stock**
- **1 cup tomatoes, peeled and cut into ½″ pieces**
- **4 cups Swiss chard, spinach or other green, julienned**
- **1 cup peas, optional**
  Salt and pepper to taste
- **4 Tbsps. grated Parmesan cheese**

elt the butter in a heavy-bottomed, high-sided sauté pan, or a wide saucepan. Add the onions, and sauté for about 10 minutes over low heat, until the onions are translucent and sweet.

While the onions are cooking, bring the stock to a boil in a small saucepan. Reduce the heat and keep the stock at a simmer.

Add the rice to the onions, and cook 3 to 5 minutes over low heat, stirring until the rice is opaque. Add 1 cup of stock and stir until it is absorbed. Add another cup of the stock and cook over low heat, stirring occasionally. Repeat with 2 more cups of stock, stirring until they are absorbed.

Meanwhile, bring a small pot of lightly salted water to a boil. Add the squash cubes and cook for about 5 minutes, until tender, but still firm — not mushy. If the peas are starchy, blanch until tender.

After all but the last 1½ cup of stock are added, add the tomatoes and squash to the rice. Cook for a few minutes. Add the peas, if using, and greens and stir until they are wilted. The risotto is done when the rice is al dente, and there is still some soupiness to the sauce. Season with salt and pepper, and sprinkle with grated Parmesan cheese.

Trade Secret: This risotto could be from northern Italy or Portugal, where the rice would be baked in a casserole. In summer or fall, "Sweet 100" cherry tomatoes would be best, but canned plum tomatoes are acceptable as well.

Joyce Goldstein
Square One Restaurant
San Francisco, California

Risotto Cakes with Wild Mushrooms

Warm the vegetable stock.
Sauté the mushrooms in olive oil until done. Set aside.

In a large pan, sauté the shallots and garlic in olive oil, then add the rice, stirring until warm. Deglaze with white wine. Season to taste.

Over low heat, continue to stir the rice while slowly adding the warm vegetable stock over a 10 minute period. This will allow the rice to absorb the stock, keeping the mixture smooth.

When the rice becomes al dente, add the sautéed mushrooms, reserving some for garnish.

When the mushrooms are warm, remove from heat and season to taste. Stir in parsley, 4 Tbsps. olive oil, and parmesan cheese to taste.

Pour mixture into a sheet pan. Cool in the refrigerator. When cold, cut out round or square pieces.

Coat with flour, then egg, then bread crumbs.

Sauté both sides until crisp. Garnish with mushrooms and herbs.

Serves 4
Preparation Time:
  30 Minutes
(note refrigeration time)

- 1 qt. vegetable stock
- 1 lb. wild mushrooms
  Olive oil
- ½ cup shallots, chopped
- 4 garlic cloves, chopped
- 6 oz. risotto rice
  (Arborio)
- 1 cup dry white wine
  Salt and pepper to taste
- 2 bunches fresh parsley, chopped
  Parmesan cheese
  Flour
- 1 egg, beaten
  Bread crumbs
  Mushrooms, herbs for garnish

Hitsch Albin
The Four Seasons
New York, New York

Risotto and Mushroom Fricassee

Serves 4
Preparation Time:
  40 Minutes

  1 shallot, chopped
  1 garlic clove, chopped
  3 Tbsps. butter
  1 Tbsp. olive oil
  1 cup Arborio rice
  ⅓ cup white wine
3½ cups vegetable stock,
     heated
  2 Tbsps. fresh herbs,
     chopped
  ¼ cup pea sprouts
  3 Tbsps. celery
     (or carrots or leeks),
     chopped
  3 Tbsps. tomato juice
  ½ lb. wild mushrooms
  1 Tbsp. corn oil
  3 Tbsps. white port wine

 weat the shallots and garlic in butter and 1 Tbsp. olive oil. Add the rice, stir, cook for 3 minutes or until the rice is opaque and evenly coated with the oil, then add the white wine. In small amounts, add the stock, ½ cup at a time. Continue to stir, allowing the rice to simmer. When the last of the stock has been added, stir in 1 Tbsp. fresh herbs, pea sprouts, vegetables and tomato juice. Continue cooking until the rice is slightly creamy and just tender, about 25 to 30 minutes total.

In a sauté pan, sauté all of the mushrooms in corn oil with 1 Tbsp. fresh herbs. Deglaze with white port wine.

Serve the risotto topped with the sautéed mushrooms.

Gray Kunz
Lespinasse
New York, New York

Risotto with Wild Mushrooms

Two hours before cooking, soak dry mushrooms in warm chicken broth.

Remove the mushrooms from broth, keep broth on the side. Squeeze the liquid from the mushrooms. Chop the mushrooms and set aside.

In a saucepan, add 2 Tbsps. butter, shallots, garlic, and all the mushrooms. Sauté for about 3 minutes on medium heat. Add ½ cup white wine, let evaporate, then add the broth you soaked the mushrooms in. Cook until reduced by half. Salt and pepper to taste and set aside.

In a saucepan, add 1 Tbsp. of butter and the rice, keep stirring for about 2 minutes. Add the remaining wine and let evaporate. Add the mushroom sauce and keep adding broth as liquid evaporates, stirring constantly for 20 minutes. When rice is soft but firm, add mascarpone, 1 Tbsp. butter and Parmesan cheese. Add salt and pepper if needed. Remove from heat, mix well and serve sprinkled with parsley.

Serves 4
Preparation Time:
   20 Minutes
(note soaking time)
Cooking Time:
   20 Minutes

- 2 oz. Porcini mushrooms, dry
- 6 cups vegetable stock
- 4 Tbsps. butter
- 1 Tbsp. shallots, chopped
- 2 garlic cloves
- 12 morel mushrooms, dry
- 4 shiitake mushrooms, fresh, sliced
- 1 cup dry white wine
  Salt and pepper to taste
- 1½ cups arborio rice, uncooked
- 1 Tbsp. mascarpone cheese
- 4 Tbsps. Parmesan cheese, grated
- 1 Tbsp. parsley, chopped

Celestino Drago
Drago
Santa Monica, California

☆

Squash and Mushroom Risotto

Serves 4
Preparation Time:
  10 Minutes
Cooking Time:
  20 Minutes

  4 Tbsps. butter
1½ cups butternut squash,
    diced
  1 onion, minced
1½ cups Arborio rice
 ⅓ lb. shiitakes, sliced
  2 leaves green cabbage,
    julienned
  1 bay leaf
    Salt and pepper to
    taste
  4 cups vegetable stock,
    hot
 ¼ cup Parmesan cheese,
    grated

eat 3 Tbsps. butter in a large saucepan and sauté squash for 5 minutes. Add the onion and cook until transparent. Add the rice and stir to coat. Add the mushrooms, cabbage, bay leaf and salt.

Stir in 2 ladles of vegetable stock. Stir and add remaining broth in 2 to 3 stages.

When rice is done and is smooth and creamy, add the remaining butter, cheese, salt and pepper. Serve immediately.

Patrick Clark
The Hay-Adams Hotel
Washington, D.C.

☆

Risotto Verde

Melt ¼ cup butter in a large sauce pan and sauté the onion until transparent. Add the rice and stir until coated with butter. Add the wine and cook until all liquid is absorbed, about 20 to 25 minutes.

Add the stock one cup at a time, stirring constantly, until each cup is absorbed.

Just after the last cup of stock, stir in the cream and spinach. Continue stirring until the mixture is creamy. Add ¼ cup of the Parmesan cheese and the remaining butter. Stir well. Season to taste.

Top with the remaining Parmesan cheese and serve.

Serves 4
Preparation Time:
  30 Minutes

½ cup (1 stick) butter
1 medium yellow onion, minced
2 cups Arborio rice
¼ cup dry white wine
4 cups vegetable stock
½ cup heavy cream
1 cup fresh spinach, washed, drained, finely chopped
½ cup grated Parmesan cheese
  Salt and pepper to taste
  Nutmeg to taste, optional

Saleh Joudeh
Saleh al Lago
Seattle, Washington
☆

Vegetable Bayaldi

Cuban Black Bean Hash

Wild Mushrooms in Brioche with Spiced Pecans

Breaded Cabbage

Stuffed Chiles, Wild Mushrooms, Saffron Sauce

Baked Eggplant Steaks with Basil & Parmesan

Red Bell Pepper Flan, Green Lentils, Rosemary Beurre Blanc

Jalapeño Corn Flan

Basil Gnocchi

Butternut Squash Gnocchi

Zucchini Ricotta Gnocchi

Vegetable Gratin with Polenta and Smoked Tomato Butter

Vegetable Lasagna

Grilled Mushrooms

Grilled Portobello Mushrooms with Tomatoes, Herb Oil

Garden Paella

Goat Cheese Potato Cake in Sabayon Sauce

Potato Lasagna of Wild Mushrooms with Herb Sauce

Mushroom & Winter Vegetable Ragout

Southeast Asian Vegetable Ragout with Rice Noodles

Oriental Rice Patties

Ratatouille Shepherd's Pie

Ranch-Style Stew with Potato Cakes

Baked Potato and Asparagus Soufflé

Blue Potato Strudel

Onion Tart

Vegetable Tart

Vidalia Onion Tart

Tofu Vegetable Roll

Layered Tortillas with Greens, Tomato and Cheese

Grilled Vegetables with Port Beurre Rouge

Vegetable Pot au Feu with Leek Vinaigrette

Steamed Vegetables in Grilled Flour Tortillas

Vegetable Tagine for Couscous

Main Courses

Vegetable Bayaldi

In a heavy sauté pan, combine the onions, 2 Tbsps. olive oil, 1 Tbsp. thyme and garlic. Stirring often, cook over very low heat until the onions are soft and tender, about 12 minutes. Do not brown. Salt and pepper to taste.

Put onions in a 9"×13" baking dish and spread them over the bottom. Arrange the tomatoes, zucchini and eggplant overlapping in alternating rows on top of the onions. Drizzle with remaining olive oil and season to taste.

Bake at 325° until vegetables are tender, about 30 minutes.

Turn oven up to 475° and sprinkle with the remaining tablespoon of thyme. Cook until the vegetables are lightly browned, about 5 more minutes. Serve immediately.

Serves 4
Preparation Time:
  10 Minutes
Cooking Time:
  40 Minutes

- 4 medium onions, finely sliced
- 6 Tbsps. olive oil
- 4 tsps. fresh thyme, chopped
- 4 garlic cloves, finely chopped
  Salt and pepper to taste
- 2 tomatoes, thinly sliced
- 1 medium zucchini, thinly sliced
- 1 eggplant, thinly sliced

Robert Holley
Brasserie le Coze
Coconut Grove, Florida

Cuban Black Bean Hash

Serves 6
Preparation Time:
  45 Minutes
Cooking Time:
  1 Hour

  8 cups black beans,
    soaked overnight
  3 bay leaves
  2 Tbsps. cumin seeds
  2 Tbsps. oregano, dried
  2 Tbsps. paprika
1½ tsps. cayenne
  ¼ cup peanut oil
  3 cups yellow onions,
    diced
  3 Tbsps. garlic, chopped
  1 Tbsp. kosher salt
  4 cups canned tomatoes
  1 Tbsp. chipotle chile,
    diced
  ¼ cup rice wine vinegar
    Jack cheese, salsa and
    tortilla chips for
    garnish

Drain and rinse beans, cover with fresh water by 2" and bring to a boil. Add bay leaves, lower heat and simmer while preparing other ingredients.

Heat a small skillet over medium heat and add the cumin and oregano, shaking pan frequently. When you begin to smell the spices, remove from heat and add paprika and cayenne. Stir once. Set aside.

In a large skillet heat the peanut oil. Add the onions and cook until softened. Add the garlic, salt, and reserved spices. Cook for 5 minutes, then add the tomatoes and chipotle chile. Simmer for 15 minutes, then add the spices to the beans. Add water if necessary.

Cook for 1 hour or until beans are softened. The beans should be creamy. Drain any excess liquid. Season to taste. Purée ⅓ of the bean mixture and add back to the remaining beans.

To make the hash, fry the bean mixture in a steel skillet with 1 Tbsp. oil over medium heat. Fry until the beans come away from the side of the pan. Top with a thin slice of jack cheese. Remove from heat when cheese has melted.

Garnish with salsa and tortilla chips.

Mike Fennelly
Mike's on the Avenue
New Orleans, Louisiana

Wild Mushrooms in Brioche with Spiced Pecans

Heat a medium-size sauté pan and melt 2 Tbsps. butter. Add mushrooms and sauté until soft. Add Marsala and reduce to a syrupy consistency. Add cream and reduce by ⅓. Finish with remaining butter. Add parsley and season to taste. Set aside.

In a cheesecloth, combine the salt, cinnamon, crushed pepper, garlic, peppercorns and coriander and tie securely, creating a brine sack.

Heat 8 cups water to a rolling boil. Add the brine sack and boil 5 to 8 minutes. Add the pecans and reduce heat to a simmer. Cook one hour.

Drain the pecans and lay out on a sheet pan, spreading evenly. Toast in the oven at 350°, checking every 10 minutes until lightly toasted. Remove from oven and blend the shelled pecans into the mushroom mixture.

Split brioches in half. Evenly distribute the mushroom-pecan mixture over the bottom half. Top with the other half of the brioche.

Serves 4
Preparation Time:
  25 Minutes
Cooking Time:
  1 Hour, 20 Minutes

- ¾ cup wild mushrooms, sliced
- ½ cup button mushrooms, sliced
- 3 Tbsps. butter
- ⅜ cup Marsala wine
- ¾ cup heavy cream
- 1 tsp. parsley, chopped
  Salt and pepper to taste
- 1 cup Kosher salt
- 1 Tbsp. cinnamon, ground
- 1 Tbsp. red pepper, crushed
- 3 garlic cloves, crushed
- 1 tsp. black peppercorns
- 1 tsp. coriander seeds, toasted
- 1½ cups pecan halves
- 4 brioches, or large rolls/buns

Anne Rosenzweig
Arcadia
New York, New York

☆

Breaded Cabbage Cutlet

Serves 6
Preparation Time:
  15 Minutes
Baking Time:
  15 Minutes

  1 **head white or Savoy
    cabbage, about 6"
    diameter**
  2 **qts. water**
  1 **Tbsp. salt**
  ½ **cup all-purpose flour**
  2 **eggs**
  2 **Tbsps. milk**
1½ **cups bread crumbs
    Salt and pepper to
    taste**
1½ **cups peanut oil
    Cheese or Bernaise
    sauce, optional
    Cherry tomatoes as
    garnish**

 n a 5 qt. pot, bring the water and salt to a rolling boil. Slice the cabbage into quarters or sixths through the core so that each slice has the core holding it together. Place the cabbage into the boiling water and cook until tender, 4 to 6 minutes.

Drain the cabbage well and place on a cloth or paper towels. Press the water out of the cabbage by placing a large baking sheet on top and weighing it down with heavy cans. Allow cabbage to cool completely.

Dust the cabbage cutlets with the flour, pat off excess. Season with salt and pepper. Beat eggs lightly with the milk. Dip each cutlet into the egg mixture. Shake off excess, then dip into the bread crumbs.

Heat the peanut oil in a large skillet. Fry until golden brown, about 3 to 4 minutes on each side.

Remove from heat and drain excess oils on paper towels.

Serve hot, topped with your favorite cheese or Bernaise sauce. Garnish with cherry tomatoes.

Fritz Blank
Deux Cheminées
Philadelphia, Pennsylvania

☆

Stuffed Chiles with Wild Mushrooms and Saffron Sauce

Roast the chiles over an open fire or under the broiler until skin blisters. Remove from heat immediately. Place chiles in a plastic bag for approximately 30 minutes, then peel the skin off. Set aside.

Sauté the peppers in hot olive oil for about 5 minutes. Add the mushrooms and cook over low heat for about 15 minutes more. Salt and pepper to taste.

Prepare the sauce in a stainless steel or copper pan. Combine the shallots, wine, vinegar and saffron. Reduce over low heat until dry.

Whisk in small pieces of butter, lemon juice, salt and pepper. Bring to a quick boil. Set aside.

With a sharp knife, make a small opening in the side of each chile and stuff with the mushroom mixture.

To serve, pour the sauce on individual serving plates and top with the roasted stuffed chiles.

Serves 4
Preparation Time:
  1 Hour

  4 Poblano chiles
  1 red bell pepper, diced
  1 green bell pepper, diced
  1 yellow bell pepper, diced
  1 lb. fresh wild mushrooms, diced
  1 Tbsp. olive oil
    Salt and pepper to taste
  2 shallots, finely chopped
  1 cup dry white wine
  ½ cup white wine vinegar
  4 threads of saffron
  2 cups butter, unsalted
    Juice of half lemon

Vincent Guerithault
Vincent Guerithault on Camelback
Phoenix, Arizona

Baked Eggplant Steaks with Basil & Parmesan

Serves 6
Preparation Time:
   25 Minutes
(note marinating time)
Baking Time:
   30 Minutes

   2 large eggplants
1½ cups basil, chopped
   2 Tbsps. garlic, minced
1¼ cups olive oil
   Salt and pepper to taste
1½ cups grated Parmesan cheese

ash and slice eggplant into ¾" thick steaks. Do not remove skin.

In a large mixing bowl combine the chopped basil, garlic, olive oil, salt and pepper. Mix well. Add the eggplant steaks to the mixture and toss well to coat. Place the eggplant steaks and the marinade in a covered container for at least 4 hours or overnight.

Remove from marinade and place steaks on an oiled sheet pan. Bake 20 to 25 minutes at 450° until eggplant becomes slightly translucent but is still firm.

Remove from the oven and cover each steak with about 1½ Tbsps. of grated cheese. Return to the oven and bake 5 minutes more, until cheese begins to melt, then broil steaks to brown the cheese. Serve hot.

Kevin Johnson
The Grange Hall
Manhattan, New York

☆

Pepper Flan with Lentils and Rosemary Beurre Blanc

O ver an open flame or under a broiler, roast the bell peppers until the skin is charred black. Peel off the skin and remove seeds. Purée in a blender.

Mix ½ cup purée with the eggs, add the cream . Butter four soufflé molds, 3 to 4 oz. each. Place molds in a baking pan and pour the purée into the soufflé molds. Fill the baking pan with hot water to reach halfway up the molds. Cover tightly with foil and bake at 300° for about 15 minutes.

Heat olive oil in a skillet. Add one chopped shallot, garlic and 1 bunch rosemary. Sweat for 2 minutes, then add the lentils and stock. Bring to a boil. Cook until tender, about 25 minutes. Salt and pepper to taste.

Heat 1 Tbsp. butter in a skillet. Sweat the remaining shallots and remaining rosemary. Add white wine and reduce to ¼ liquid. Add the cream and reduce again to ¼ liquid. Slowly whisk in the remaining butter, one cube at a time. Strain.

To serve, arrange the lentils on one end of each serving plate in a circle. Unmold the soufflé in the center of the plate and spoon the sauce around the soufflé. Serve hot.

Serves 4
Preparation Time:
 1 Hour
Cooking Time:
 40 Minutes

 3 **red bell peppers**
 2 **eggs**
 ⅓ **cup cream**
 1 **Tbsp. olive oil**
 1 **shallot, chopped**
 1 **garlic clove, chopped**
 2 **bunches rosemary, chopped**
 ½ **cup lentils**
 1 **cup vegetable stock**
 ¾ **cup (1½ sticks) butter, cubed**
 6 **shallots, chopped**
 1 **cup white wine**
 1 **Tbsp. heavy cream**

Thierry Rautureau
Rover's
Seattle, Washington

Jalapeño Corn Flan

Serves 6
Preparation Time:
  30 Minutes
Cooking Time:
  30 Minutes

10 **large ears sweet corn**
 2 **tomatoes, peeled,**
    seeded, finely chopped
 2 **jalapeño chiles, finely**
    chopped
 4 **eggs, lightly beaten**
    Juice of 2 limes
 1 **Tbsp. maple syrup**
    Salt to taste

 huck and clean each ear of corn. Remove the kernels with a sharp knife. Reserve 1½ cups corn kernels. Scrape off the pulp of each cob with dull side of knife. Mix together with remaining kernels.

Purée the pulp mixture in a food processor. Strain the pulp through a fine strainer, reserving the corn milk, yielding about 2 cups. Discard pulp.

Heat the corn milk in a small saucepan over medium heat, stirring constantly until thickened, about 8 minutes. Remove the mixture from the heat and cool the liquid in a medium-size bowl. When the mixture is cool, add the reserved corn, tomatoes, jalapeños, eggs, lime juice, maple syrup and salt. Stir to combine and pour the mixture into six 4 oz. oiled molds.

Put molds in a pan filled with 1" warm water. Place pan carefully into heated oven and cook at 350° for about 30 minutes. When fully cooked, the flan should feel firm.

Dean Fearing
The Mansion on Turtle Creek
Dallas, Texas

Basil Gnocchi

I n a saucepan, bring the water, butter and salt to a rolling boil. Add flour and mix with a wooden spoon until mixture forms a loose ball. Transfer the mixture to a mixing bowl.

Using an electric mixer with dough hook attachment, mix on low speed until dough cools. With machine running, add one egg at a time until dough is well mixed. Season with nutmeg, pepper and basil.

Coat a shallow casserole dish with olive oil.

Bring about ½ gallon water to a rolling boil.

Fill pastry bag with ½" round tip with the gnocchi mixture.

Hold pastry bag over boiling water and squeeze while cutting dough into 1" pieces with a small knife. Simmer about 2 minutes, then remove with a slotted spoon. Transfer into the flat casserole dish. Repeat with the remaining mixture.

Add cream or tomato sauce, sprinkle with cheese and bake for 12 to 15 minutes at 375° or until brown.

Trade Secret: This dish may be served as an appetizer or with a salad as a main course.

Serves 4
Preparation Time:
  25 Minutes
Baking Time:
  15 Minutes

  1 **cup water**
  2 **Tbsps. butter**
  2 **tsps. salt**
  1 **cup all-purpose flour**
  4 **eggs, large**
  ⅛ **tsp. ground nutmeg**
  ⅛ **tsp. white pepper**
  2 **Tbsps. fresh basil,**
    chopped
  1 **Tbsp. olive oil**
  1 **cup tomato sauce or**
    cream sauce
    Grated cheese for
    garnish, optional

Kaspar Donier
Kaspar's
Seattle, Washington

Butternut Squash Gnocchi with Butter and Sage

Serves 6
Preparation Time:
  30 Minutes
Cooking Time:
  1 Hour

  2 lbs. butternut squash
    Olive oil
    Salt and pepper to
    taste
  1 lb. potatoes
  1 egg, beaten
  ½ cup Parmesan, grated
  1 tsp. salt
  ¼ tsp. ground pepper
  1 cup flour
  ½ cup (1 stick) butter,
    melted
    Sage leaves
    Grated Parmesan
    cheese as garnish

ut squash in half and remove seeds. Rub with olive oil, salt and pepper. Roast flesh side down on a sheet pan at 400° for 45 to 60 minutes. Remove from oven and cool to handling temperature.

Remove flesh and put through a food mill or food processor until smooth.

While squash roasts, peel, quarter and boil the potatoes until just cooked. Cool and coarsely process in a food mill or processor.

Combine the potatoes, squash, egg, Parmesan, salt and pepper. Mix well by hand. Gently work in flour until incorporated. Dough will be soft and a little sticky. Do not add more flour.

Bring 4 qts. of salted water to a boil. Place dough in a pastry bag with a large, round tip and cut gnocchi at 1" intervals into the boiling water about 12 at a time. Cook 1 to 2 minutes after they rise to the surface. Remove with a slotted spoon and set aside to drain. Repeat until all dough is used.

Melt butter in a sauté pan with the sage leaves and toss the gnocchi in the mixture. Serve in bowls sprinkled with freshly grated Parmesan and black pepper.

Trade Secret: This gnocchi is also good with a sauce of cream and Gruyère cheese.

Christopher Israel
Zefiro
Portland, Oregon

Zucchini Ricotta Gnocchi

Grate the zucchini, then place in a colander and toss with the Kosher salt. Allow to drain for 20 to 30 minutes. Wrap in cheesecloth and squeeze tightly to remove as much moisture as possible.

Combine the zucchini with the ricotta, egg, yolk, Parmesan, salt and pepper. Mix well. Gently mix in the flour. Do not overwork the dough. Let the mixture rest for 30 minutes in the refrigerator.

Bring a pot of water to boil with a little salt.

Divide the dough into fourths. Working on a floured surface, gently roll into ropes about 1" thick, and cut at 1" intervals.

Place the dough in the boiling water and boil for 1 to 2 minutes after they rise to the surface. Check one piece to insure they are cooked through. Remove with a slotted spoon and set aside to drain.

Toss the gnocchi in melted butter and serve in bowls sprinkled with diced tomato, Parmesan and basil leaves.

Trade Secret: This gnocchi is also delicious with fresh tomato sauce.

Serves 6
Preparation Time:
 20 Minutes
(note refrigeration time)

1½ lbs. zucchini
 2 Tbsps. Kosher salt
1½ cups ricotta cheese
 1 egg
 1 egg yolk
 ½ cup Parmesan, grated
 1 tsp. salt
 ½ tsp. pepper
1½ cups flour
 2 Tbsps. fresh basil, chopped
   Melted butter
 1 tomato, seeded, diced
   Basil leaves

Christopher Israel
Zefiro
Portland, Oregon

123

Vegetable Gratin with Polenta and Smoked Tomato Butter

Serves 4
Preparation Time:
  30 Minutes
Baking Time:
  30 Minutes

  1 **cup milk**
  2 **cups water**
  1 **cup polenta or stone-
    ground corn meal**
  ½ **tsp. salt**
  2 **Tbsps. butter, softened
    Fresh herbs (basil,
    rosemary or sage),
    chopped**
  2 **red peppers, roasted,
    peeled, seeded, cut
    into strips**
  2 **garlic bulbs, roasted,
    peeled**
  1 **eggplant, peeled, cut
    into ½″ dice**
  ½ **lb. mushrooms**
  2 **cans artichoke hearts,
    quartered, drained,
    sliced**
  2 **zucchini, sliced
    lengthwise into ⅛″
    ribbons**
  1 **bunch fresh spinach,
    washed, stemmed**
  ½ **cup grated Parmesan
    or Fontina cheese**

I n a medium heavy-bottomed pot, bring milk and water to a boil, then sprinkle in the polenta, whisking constantly. Keep whisking or stirring until mixture boils and thickens. Reduce heat and simmer for about 10 to 15 minutes, stirring occasionally. Add the salt, butter and herbs.

Pour into a 8″ square baking pan brushed with olive oil or butter. Smooth into an even layer about ¼″ to ½″ thick. Let cool.

Separately, sauté the eggplant and artichoke hearts, and wilt the spinach, in olive oil.

Alternate layers of the peppers, garlic, eggplant, mushrooms, artichoke hearts, zucchini and spinach, pressing down firmly on each layer and ending with the red peppers.

Top with cheese and bake at 350° for about 30 minutes. Cut into squares and serve.

Trade Secret: Serve with Susan Spicer's Smoked Tomato Butter, page 188.

Susan Spicer
Bayona
New Orleans, Louisiana

Vegetable Lasagna

Coat the bottom and sides of the loaf pan with 1 tsp. olive oil. Using half the vegetables, layer the bottom of the pan with zucchini, salt, pepper and onion slices. Then layer the yellow squash, salt, pepper, and garlic slices.

Using all the slices, layer the potato, salt and pepper. Drizzle with 1 tsp. olive oil.

Sprinkle on 4 teaspoons of Parmesan/Romano cheese blend. Layer all the eggplant slices, salt and pepper. Add 3 teaspoons fresh basil and 2 teaspoons fresh oregano. Put the tomato slices in the center of the pan in a row. Place the yellow squash in an outside layer. Layer the onion slices, basil, salt, and pepper. Layer the zucchini, salt and pepper. Add 1 tsp. olive oil. Layer the Mozzarella cheese on top. Pour the stock over the vegetable lasagna. Place the foil over the top, seal tightly. Bake at 375° for 30 minutes.

Trade Secret: Traditional lasagna takes on a new look when fresh vegetables are laced with a low fat cheese. In addition to adding fiber to the diet, fresh vegetables are packed with plenty of vitamins and minerals.

Serves 6
Preparation Time:
  30 Minutes
Baking Time:
  30 Minutes

- 3 tsps. olive oil
- 2 small zucchini, sliced
  Salt and pepper to taste
- 1 small onion, sliced
- 2 small yellow squash, sliced
- 3 small garlic cloves, sliced
- 1 medium potato, sliced
- 2 Tbsps. Parmesan/Romano cheese blend
- 1 small eggplant, sliced
- ½ bunch basil, chopped (or ¼ tsp. dried basil)
- 1 stem oregano, chopped (or ¼ tsp. dried oregano)
- 3 tomatoes, sliced
- 3 oz. Mozzarella cheese, sliced
- 2 cups vegetable stock

Emeril Lagasse
Emeril's
New Orleans, Louisiana

✬

Grilled Mushrooms

Serves 6
Preparation Time:
 10 Minutes
(note marinating time)

3 lbs. mushrooms, whole
   (bolete, portobello or
   shiitake)
½ bunch parsley,
   chopped
4 garlic cloves, minced
   Juice and zest of 1 lime
2 chipotle chiles,
   seedless, chopped
3 Tbsps. olive oil
   Salt and pepper to
   taste

ick stems off mushrooms and slice lengthwise ½" thick.

In a large mixing bowl toss mushroom tops and stems with the remaining ingredients. Marinate 4 to 6 hours at room temperature or overnight in refrigerator.

Grill 2 to 3 minutes each side. Season to taste with salt and pepper.

Trade Secret: This dish is exceptional if grilled over wood or wood briquettes. Serve in the center of a plate, splashed with vegetable pestos and Potato Tumbleweeds on page 166.

Peter Zimmer
Inn of the Anasazi
Santa Fe, New Mexico

Portobello Mushrooms with Tomato Salad

Remove stems from the mushrooms. Cut the garlic into small slivers. Make a series of tiny incisions in the tops of the mushrooms, using the tip of a paring knife. Insert the slivers of garlic. Marinate the mushrooms with the chile oil, chopped garlic, chopped herbs, salt and pepper for at least 2 hours.

For the herb oil: Quickly puree the olive oil, shallot, black pepper, basil and parsley in a blender, salting to taste. Strain the mixture through a fine mesh strainer. In a saucepan over low heat, bring the balsamic vinegar, rosemary and 3 Tbsps. of the herb marinade to a boil.

Grill or pan roast the portobellos, basting with herb oil. Arrange the greens on the plates or a platter. Layer with the tomatoes and top with the mushrooms. Drizzle the herb oil over the salad.

Serves 4
Preparation Time:
  25 Minutes
(note marinating time)

- 4 portobello mushrooms
- 2 garlic cloves
- 1 Tbsp. chile oil
- 1 Tbsp. chopped garlic
- 3 Tbsps. your choice of herbs, chopped
  Salt and black pepper to taste
- 1½ cups olive oil
- 1 shallot, peeled
  Black pepper, cracked
- 1 bunch basil
- 1 bunch parsley
- 3 tomatoes, peeled, seeded, diced
- 1 bunch arugula or other greens
- ¼ cup balsamic vinegar
- ½ tsp. fresh rosemary, chopped

Mark Militello
Mark's Place
North Miami, Florida

☆

Garden Paella

Serves 4
Preparation Time:
 45 Minutes
Cooking Time:
 30 Minutes

¼ cup olive oil
1 large onion, chopped
1 red pepper, chopped
3 garlic cloves, crushed
½ tsp. thyme
¼ tsp. oregano
2 bay leaves, whole
  Salt and pepper to
  taste
1½ cups short grain rice
3½ cups vegetable stock
  Pinch of saffron
  strands
1 zucchini, cut into ¼"
  slices
1 summer squash, cut
  into ¼" slices
6 broccoli florettes
4 cherry tomatoes
2 artichoke hearts,
  quartered
¼ cup small green peas
  for garnish

 n a large pan, heat olive oil and sauté onion, red pepper and garlic. Add thyme, oregano, bay leaves, salt and pepper.

In a paella pan or similar pan, heat 1 Tbsp. oil. Brown rice until coated and opaque. Add mixture from the first pan. Mix well.

Add saffron to vegetable stock. Place in paella pan and bring to a boil. Lower heat. Arrange zucchini, summer squash, broccoli, tomatoes and artichoke hearts on top of rice. Cover and simmer for 20 minutes.

Uncover, add peas, and simmer for 5 more minutes. Let settle for a few minutes before serving.

Trade Secret: To best extract the flavor from saffron, wrap it in foil and keep it in a warm place to dry. Then mix with warm stock.

Mario Leon-Iriarte
Dali
Somerville, Massachusetts

Goat Cheese Potato Cake in Sabayon Sauce

Cook the potatoes in boiling water until tender. Remove from heat, cool, peel and cut into slices or dices of medium size. In a mixer, blend the potatoes with the olives, ½ tsp. tarragon, thyme, olive oil, cream, vinegar, salt and pepper.

Fill a ring mold, 2½″×1½″ (or a small baking dish) ¾ full with potato mixture. Top with the tomato sauce in a very thin layer and finish filling mold with the crumbled goat cheese.

Heat in the oven at 350° for about 15 minutes, or until warmed through.

Over a low heat or a double boiler, whip the eggs and the wine until soft peaks form. Season with the remaining tarragon, salt and pepper.

Trade Secret: The Sabayon can be spooned over the top of the cake and browned quickly under a broiler.

Serves 6
Preparation Time:
  20 Minutes
Cooking Time:
  20 Minutes

- 3 large yellow potatoes
- 8 black olives, finely chopped
- 1 tsp. fresh tarragon, chopped
- ½ tsp. fresh thyme, chopped
- ¼ cup olive oil
- 2 Tbsps. cream
- 2 Tbsps. sherry vinegar
  Salt and pepper to taste
- 1 tsp. tomato sauce
- 2 oz. goat cheese
- 2 egg yolks
- 2 Tbsps. white wine

Robert Holley
Brasserie le Coze
Coconut Grove, Florida
☆

Potato Lasagna of Wild Mushrooms with Herb Sauce

Serves 4
Preparation Time:
  30 Minutes

  4 **large Idaho potatoes**
  ½ **cup (1 stick) butter**
  ⅓ **cup shiitake**
    mushrooms, chopped
  ⅓ **cup oyster**
    mushrooms, chopped
  ⅓ **cup white mushrooms,**
    chopped
  ⅓ **cup chanterelles,**
    chopped, optional
  1 **large shallot, chopped**
    fine
  ¾ **cup celery broth**
  ½ **bunch parsley,**
    chopped
  1 **Roma tomato, diced**

ut the potatoes in rectangular shapes of 3″×1½″. Slice each potato into cubes in 5 slices. Place the slices on a buttered sheet pan and bake in the oven at 300° for a few minutes until soft.

Sauté the mushrooms in half the butter over low heat. Add the shallot and cook until soft. Set aside.

Warm the celery broth over medium heat until broth begins to reduce. Add remaining butter to the broth in a blender and finish with the parsley and tomatoes.

In 4 alternate layers, place the potato slices and the mushrooms in a loaf type pan. To serve, place the potato lasagna in a soup plate and cover with the warm herb sauce.

Joachim Splichal
Patina
Los Angeles, California

☆

Mushroom & Winter Vegetable Ragout with Soft Polenta

P repare a quick mushroom stock by combining the dried shiitake mushrooms, a few sprigs of fresh herbs, ½ yellow onion, 4 garlic cloves, cold water, soy sauce and a pinch of salt to a boil. Simmer over low heat while cooking the polenta. Cook for 30 minutes, strain stock and discard vegetables. Set aside for ragout.

Allow 20 minutes to cook the polenta. Whisk polenta into boiling salted water and whisk vigorously until polenta dissolves. Turn down the heat and continue to stir so polenta does not stick to bottom of the pan. Cook over medium heat until the grains dissolve completely and the polenta is smooth, about 20 minutes. Add ¼ cup butter, salt and pepper. When the polenta is done, leave over low flame and stir occasionally until ready to serve. Thin with hot water if it begins to thicken. Add half of the cheese just before serving and sprinkle the rest of the cheese over the polenta when it is served.

Sauté 1 medium yellow onion in 2 Tbsps. butter and olive oil with 4 minced garlic cloves and salt and pepper until soft. Add half of the wine and reduce. Add the mushrooms, turnips, fennel and peppers. Season with a few splashes of soy sauce. Add more butter and olive oil as necessary, the remaining wine and just enough mushroom stock to make a sauce. Cook the vegetables until tender and flavorful.

Finish seasoning with fresh herbs, salt and pepper. Add creme fraiche or sour cream to lightly bind the sauce. Serve with soft polenta.

Trade Secret: Mushrooms that work well in this dish are fresh shiitake, chanterelle or porcini mushrooms. If using fresh shiitake mushrooms, use only the caps for the ragout.

Annie Somerville
Greens
San Francisco, California

Serves 6
Preparation Time:
  1 Hour

  3 oz. dried shiitake
    mushrooms
    A few sprigs of fresh
    herbs
1½ medium yellow
    onions, diced large
  8 garlic cloves
  2 cups cold water
  ¼ cup soy sauce
  1 cup polenta
  4 cups boiling salted
    water
  ½ cup butter
    Salt and black pepper
    to taste
  ½ lb. Parmesan cheese,
    grated
  2 Tbsps. olive oil
  1 cup red wine
  1 lb. mushrooms, sliced
    thick
  1 large turnip, cut into
    ½" cubes
  2 fennel bulbs, sliced
    thick
  1 medium red pepper,
    sliced thick
  1 medium yellow
    pepper, sliced thick
1½ cups fresh herbs,
    (parsley, marjoram,
    oregano, chives)
  ¼ cup sour cream or
    creme fraiche

Southeast Asian Vegetable Ragout with Flat Rice Noodles

Serves 4
Preparation Time:
30 Minutes

- ½ lb. flat rice noodles
- 1 bunch asparagus
- 1 yellow bell pepper, chopped
- 2 red bell peppers, chopped
- ½ lb. oyster mushrooms, chopped
- ¼ lb. pea pods
- ¼ lb. sugar snap peas
- 1 tsp. ground ginger
- 1 Tbsp. peanut oil
- 3 Tbsps. sesame oil
- ½ cup lime juice
  Zest of 4 limes
- ⅓ cup light soy sauce
- ¼ cup lemon juice
- 2 tsps. salt
- 4 tsps. pepper
- ⅓ cup fresh ginger, finely chopped
- 1 cup fresh basil, finely chopped
- 8 tsps. chile oil
- 1½ cups coconut milk, canned
- ½ cup coriander
- 3 Tbsps. cashews, roasted, coarsely chopped

ring a large saucepan of water to a boil, remove from heat and add the rice noodles. Let sit for about 15 minutes, then drain and immerse in cold water. Set aside.

Stir fry the asparagus, yellow pepper, red peppers, mushrooms, pea pods, sugar snaps and ground ginger in the peanut oil and ½ Tbsp. sesame oil. Set aside.

Prepare the sauce by combining all the remaining ingredients except the cashews.

Drain the noodles thoroughly and toss with the vegetables and sauce. Garnish with the cashews and serve.

Roxsand Suarez
Roxsand
Phoenix, Arizona

Oriental Rice Patties

In a mixing bowl, stir together the cooked rice, sour cream or yogurt, and chopped scallions. Stir in the eggs one at a time. Add the remaining ingredients except the bread crumbs. Stir in bread crumbs ¼ cup at a time until mixture is of a consistency to easily make patties. The amount of bread crumbs may vary depending on the dryness of the rice. Make all patties and set aside until ready to cook.

Toast each patty in an oiled pan until golden brown.

To serve, top with additional yogurt or sour cream.

Trade Secret: A tasty accompaniment to the rice patties is a red bell pepper purée.

Serves 6
Preparation Time:
  15 Minutes

  3 cups cooked rice
  ½ cup sour cream or
    yogurt
  1 bunch scallions,
    chopped
  3 eggs
  ½ tsp. Tabasco
  ½ tsp. light soy sauce
    Salt & cayenne pepper
    to taste
    Black bean paste,
    optional
  1 tsp. red chile flakes
  ¾ cup bread crumbs

David Beckwith
Central 159
Pacific Grove, California

☆

Ratatouille Shepherd's Pie

Serves 4
Preparation Time:
 40 Minutes

¾ cup olive oil
2 Japanese eggplants,
  ¼" diced
  Salt and pepper to
  taste
2 small zucchini, diced
1 small fennel bulb,
  diced
1 red bell pepper,
  roasted, diced
1 red onion, diced
3 garlic cloves, chopped
2 medium Roma
  tomatoes, diced
3 Tbsps. basil, chopped
1⅛ tsps. thyme, chopped
1 lb. spinach, julienned
1 Tbsp. butter
⅔ cup bread crumbs, fine
¼ cup Parmesan cheese,
  grated
1 cup potatoes, mashed
  Thyme sprigs
  Black olives

Heat 1 Tbsp. olive oil in a non-stick pan. Sauté the eggplant until tender. Season to taste and drain.

Sauté the zucchini, fennel and bell pepper, seasoning to taste and draining.

Sauté the onion in another tablespoon of olive oil, cooking until soft. Add 2 cloves of garlic and the tomatoes. Season to taste. Cook over low heat until all liquid is evaporated. Add the cooked vegetables and stir in the basil and 1 tsp. thyme. Season and cool.

Blanch the spinach strips and squeeze dry.

Melt the butter in a sauté pan, sauté the spinach until hot. Season and drain on a paper towel.

Combine the bread crumbs, cheese and remaining thyme. Stir remaining garlic into the mashed potatoes.

Place a 3¼" ring on each of 4 heat-proof plates. Divide the spinach among the four rings, pressing down to form a layer. Spoon the ratatouille into each mold. Fill them ¾ full. Finish each mold with the garlic mashed potatoes and sprinkle the crumb mixture on top.

Heat 5 minutes at 250°, then brown under a broiler.

Remove the rings and absorb any juices with paper towels. Garnish with a sprig of thyme, black olives and olive oil.

Patrick Clark
The Hay-Adams Hotel
Washington, D.C.

✩

Ranch-Style Stew with Potato Cakes

Peel the potatoes and simmer in salted water until tender, 20 to 30 minutes. Drain and cool completely, then grate. Mix the potatoes, egg yolk, 4 cloves minced garlic, cheese, thyme and 1 tsp. salt. Form into 3" diameter, ½" thick cakes.

In a deep plate, mix the eggs, milk and ½ tsp. salt. Place the flour and bread crumbs in separate deep plates. Dip both sides of cakes into flour, then egg mixture, then bread crumbs. Firmly coat all sides.

In a food processor blend the blackened tomatillos to a coarse puree. Set aside.

In a large saucepan, over medium heat, heat olive oil. Add the onion and cook, stirring regularly, until onions begin to brown, 7 to 8 minutes. Add the remaining garlic, 2 cloves, and cook 2 minutes. Add the tomatillo puree and boil quickly, stirring, until thick, about 5 minutes. Add the stock, parsley, and 1 tsp. salt. Simmer, partially covered, for 30 minutes. Remove the parsley. Thin, if necessary, to consistency of a light broth.

In a large skillet, heat ¼ cup oil over medium-high heat. When hot, lay the cakes in a single layer. Fry both sides until golden brown and crispy. Drain on paper towels and keep warm. Repeat with remaining cakes, adding more oil if necessary.

Add the mushrooms, Poblano chile, carrots and green beans. Simmer over medium heat until vegetables are tender, 8 to 10 minutes.

To serve, pour stew in soup bowls with 2 potato cakes per bowl. Garnish with a sprig of parsley.

Rick Bayless
Topolobampo, Frontera Grill & Zinfandel
Chicago, Illinois

Serves 4
Preparation Time:
 1 Hour
Cooking Time:
 1 Hour

- 2 lbs. red potatoes
- 1 egg yolk
- 6 garlic cloves, minced
- ½ cup Parmesan cheese
- 1 tsp. dried, or
  1½ Tbsps. fresh, thyme
- 2½ tsps. salt
- 2 eggs, beaten
- 2 Tbsps. milk
- ⅓ cup flour
- ¾ cup bread crumbs, dried
- 1½ lbs. tomatillos, broiled
- 1 Tbsp. olive oil
- 1 medium onion, sliced
- 2 cups vegetable stock, or water or tomato juice
- 1 large sprig Italian parsley
- ¼ cup oil for frying
- 1 cup wild mushrooms, sliced, cut to ¾" pieces
- 1 large Poblano chile, broiled, peeled, seeded, sliced
- 2 large carrots, sliced diagonally
- 1 cup green beans, ends snipped
  Italian parsley for garnish

Baked Potato and Asparagus Soufflé

Serves 4
Preparation Time:
  40 Minutes
Baking Time:
  1½ Hours

  3 **baking potatoes, large**
  1 **tsp. butter**
  ¼ **cup fresh bread**
     crumbs or grated
     cheese
  1 **cup sliced asparagus,**
     cooked
  ½ **cup asparagus tips,**
     cooked
  1 **cup butter, room**
     temperature
  4 **eggs, separated**
  ½ **cup heavy cream**
     Salt and pepper to
     taste
  ¼ **cup grated Parmesan**
     cheese, optional

ake the potatoes at 350° for 45-60 minutes, until done. Set aside.

Coat the inside of a 2 qt. soufflé dish with butter and bread crumbs or cheese.

Scoop out the hot baked potatoes into a food processor. Add 1 cup asparagus and pulse the processor until the vegetables are puréed and smooth. Set aside. Reserve ½ cup asparagus tips as a garnish.

In a separate bowl, cream the butter until light and fluffy. Whisk in the egg yolks one at a time. Whisk in the cream. Mix in the puréed vegetables.

In a separate bowl beat the egg whites until stiff peaks form.

Carefully fold together the vegetables and egg whites. Reserved asparagus tips may be added now or use them as a final garnish after the soufflé is cooked.

Fill the soufflé dish and bake at 350° for about 30 minutes, until golden.

Serve immediately.

Fritz Blank
Deux Cheminées
Philidelphia, Pennsylvania

Blue Potato Strudel

 Scrub the potatoes well, rub in olive oil and bake at 450° about 30 minutes or until tender. Remove from oven to cool.

Sauté the onion in ¼ cup butter until translucent. Season with salt and pepper. Set aside to cool slightly.

In a food processor combine the potatoes, salt and pepper, parsley, chives, ricotta cheese and egg until well mixed. Season to taste.

Lay out filo dough sheets carefully, keeping those not in use covered with a damp cloth. Melt the remaining butter, brush one filo sheet with the melted butter. Lay a second sheet down. Place ½ cup of the potato mixture on the bottom third of the filo. Fold the left and right thirds over, then roll up. You will have a rectangular shape. Brush with butter. Repeat with the remaining sheets.

Bake at 350° about 15 minutes or until golden brown.

Trade Secret: Serve with black bean sauce on page 171 and fig slaw on page 77.

Serves 6
Preparation Time:
  30 Minutes
Baking Time:
  45 Minutes

  3 **large blue Peruvian potatoes**
    Olive oil
  1 **large onion, diced**
  ¼ **cup butter (½ stick), melted**
  1 **tsp. salt**
  ½ **tsp. pepper**
  2 **Tbsps. fresh parsley, chopped**
  2 **Tbsps. chives, chopped**
  7 **Tbsps. butter**
  ½ **cup ricotta cheese**
  1 **egg**
    Filo dough, pre-made

Roxsand Suarez
Roxsand
Phoenix, Arizona

☆

Onion Tart

Serves 8
Preparation Time:
  30 Minutes
Cooking Time:
  1 Hour

 8" tart shell, pre-baked
 6 large yellow onions,
   finely chopped
¼ cup olive oil
 2 Tbsps. fresh thyme,
   chopped
 1 Tbsp. garlic, chopped
¼ cup sherry vinegar
   Salt and pepper to
   taste
 1 cup heavy cream
 5 eggs
 4 oz. Gruyère cheese

n a sauté pan on low heat, combine the onion, olive oil, thyme and garlic. Stir slowly and cook until tender, about 20 minutes. Do not brown. When onions are cooked add the vinegar and season to taste.

Mix together the eggs and cream. Season with salt and pepper. Fold cream into the onion mixture.

Place a thin layer of gruyere cheese in the bottom of a tart shell. Spoon in the onion mixture.

Cover with foil and bake at 375° for 30 minutes. Remove the foil and bake another 10 minutes to brown the top.

Trade Secret: Slice and serve with mixed greens and your favorite vinaigrette.

Robert Holley
Brasserie le Coze
Coconut Grove, Florida

Vegetable Tart with Sweet Peppers and Basil Oils

S auté the onions and garlic in 2 Tbsps. olive oil for two minutes, add the tomato juice, oregano, thyme and ⅛ tsp. basil and simmer 3 minutes. Add couscous, cover and remove from heat until ready to assemble tart.

In a blender, purée the yellow pepper. Slowly add ½ cup olive oil, salt and pepper to taste. Set aside. Repeat the same procedure with the red pepper. Purée ½ cup basil in a blender while adding ½ cup olive oil. Store all flavored oils covered until ready.

Sauté the potatoes in olive oil until they are golden brown on both sides and cooked through. Set aside. Sauté the spinach in olive oil until just cooked. Salt and pepper to taste. Set aside. Sauté the zucchini and summer squash until soft, about 3 minutes.

Arrange the cooked potato slices in a spiral in two individual-sized oven-proof molds. Top with equal amounts of the spinach, then the zucchini. Top each one with 3 to 4 Tbsps. of the couscous. For the final layer, place the summer squash in a spiral on top of the couscous.

Bake at 375° for 5 minutes, until warm through. To serve, top each tart with 1 Tbsp. of chopped tomatoes. Drizzle all three oils around the tart artfully.

Trade Secret: Flavored oils may be prepared two days ahead.

Serves 2
Preparation Time:
  1½ Hours

  3 Tbsps. onion, chopped
  1 tsp. garlic, chopped
1¾ cups olive oil
  1 cup tomato juice
  ⅛ tsp. oregano
  ⅛ tsp. thyme
  ½ cup + ⅛ tsp. basil
  1 cup couscous
  1 yellow bell pepper, roasted, skinned, seeded
    Salt and pepper to taste
  1 red bell pepper, roasted, skinned & seeded
  1 or 2 medium potatoes, very thinly sliced
    Oil for sautéing
  ½ lb. spinach, washed
  1 zucchini, thinly sliced
  1 summer squash, thinly sliced
  2 Tbsps. tomato chopped

Alex Daglis
The Place at Yesterday's
Newport, Rhode Island

☆

Vidalia Onion Tart

Serves 6
Preparation Time:
  40 Minutes
(note refrigeration time)
Baking Time:
  25 Minutes

  2 cups flour
  ⅛ tsp. salt
  1½ cups butter (3 sticks),
    chilled, cut into small
    pieces
  ¼ cup ice water
  3 Vidalia onions,
    chopped
  1 cup heavy cream
  1 egg
  1 egg yolk
    Salt and pepper,
    Nutmeg and cumin
    seeds to taste

ake the tart by placing the flour and salt into a mixing bowl. Add the butter and work into the flour. Add the water and form into dough. Do not overwork the dough. Chill for at least 2 hours.

Roll out the dough to ⅛″ thick and fit into a pie pan. Prick dough all over with a fork. Set aside.

Prepare the filling by sautéing the onions in butter until tender. Add the cream and reduce until thickened. Mix in eggs and season with salt, pepper and nutmeg to taste. Pour filling into pie shell. Sprinkle cumin on top.

Bake at 400° for 25 minutes at the bottom of the oven until done.

Guenter Seeger
The Ritz-Carlton, Buckhead
Atlanta, Georgia

Tofu Vegetable Roll

Trim the ends from eggplant, zucchini and carrot. Cut each lengthwise into paper-thin slices. Cut the cores from the cabbage leaves and discard, leaving each leaf in 2 pieces. Cut the leek in half through the root.

Bring a large pot of water to a boil and cook the leek and cabbage until soft, about 5 minutes. Drain and pat dry. Cut the root off the leek and separate the leaves.

Place a bamboo sushi mat (or damp dish towel, napkin or several layers of cheesecloth) on your work surface. Arrange the eggplant strips on it in a layer, slightly overlapping. Next spread the tofu over the eggplant. Top with alfalfa sprouts over the bottom ⅔ of the tofu. Arrange the bell pepper strips on top, running left to right, covering the sprouts in a single layer.

Starting at the bottom of the mat, tightly roll up the vegetables into a cylinder. Squeeze hard to eliminate excess liquid. Peel away the mat and set the roll aside.

Return the mat to the work surface. Cover the mat with leek strips. Follow with a layer of carrots and the blanched cabbage leaves. Over that, place the scallions, followed by zucchini. Spread the remaining sprouts over the upper third of the zucchini and the remaining tofu over the bottom ⅔.

Put the eggplant-encased roll over the tofu. Once again, roll up the vegetables in the mat, with the first roll inside. Squeeze to eliminate liquid. Remove the mat and wrap tightly in several layers of plastic wrap. Refrigerate until ready to cook.

Bring water to a boil in the bottom of a steamer or wok. Place the roll on the steamer basket. Cover and steam for 5 to 6 minutes.

Trade Secret: This recipe is served at The Four Seasons with Gado-Gado Peanut Sauce on page 174.

Serves 8
Preparation Time:
  45 Minutes

- 1 small Japanese eggplant
- 1 small zucchini
- 1 small carrot, peeled
- ½ small head green cabbage
- 1 small leek
- 1 small bunch scallions
- 2 oz. tofu, cut into ¼" cubes
  Alfalfa sprouts
- 1 small red bell pepper, cut into ¼" strips
- 1 small green bell pepper, cut into ¼" strips
- 1 small yellow bell pepper, cut into ¼" strips

Hitsch Albin
The Four Seasons
New York, New York

Layered Tortillas with Greens, Tomato and Cheese

Serves 8
Preparation Time:
  30 Minutes
Baking Time:
  40 Minutes

  4 **cups spinach, or Swiss**
    chard leaves, washed,
    dried
  2 **medium zucchini,**
    ¼″ diced
    Salt to taste
    Oil for frying
 24 **corn tortillas**
    Chipotle chiles to
    taste, optional
  5 **cups tomato-chipotle**
    sauce, see page 187
  4 **cups Monterey Jack**
    cheese, or other
    melting cheese, grated
 1½ **cups corn kernels**
  ⅓ **cup fresh cilantro,**
    chopped

 ring water to a boil in a steamer. Put the greens into the steamer basket, cover and steam until just tender, 2 to 3 minutes. Spread them out on a baking sheet to cool.

When cooled, roughly chop steamed greens.

Steam the diced zucchini until just tender, 2 to 3 minutes. Spread out to cool. Sprinkle zucchini and greens with salt.

Pour a thin coating of oil in a small skillet and heat over medium heat. Line a baking sheet with several layers of paper towels. When the oil is hot, quick-fry the tortillas one at a time for a few seconds per side, just to soften them, not to fry crisp. Drain tortillas in a single layer on paper towels immediately. Blot dry.

Lightly grease a 9″×13″ baking dish. Spread a thin layer of tomato sauce over the bottom of the pan, then lay out 6 tortillas in a single layer to cover the sauce. Evenly spread the greens and ¼ of the remaining sauce and cheese. Add another layer of tortillas. Spread the corn and ⅓ of the remaining sauce and cheese. Top with another layer of tortillas and the zucchini. Spread on ½ of the remaining sauce and cheese. Add a final layer of tortillas and the remaining sauce and cheese.

Cover lightly with foil and bake at 350° for 25 minutes. Uncover and bake for 10 to 15 minutes more, until bubbling and lightly browned. Sprinkle with chopped cilantro and serve.

Rick Bayless
Topolobampo, Frontera Grill & Zinfandel
Chicago, Illinois

Grilled Vegetables with Port Beurre Rouge

Prepare the port beurre rouge by combining the vinegar, port and shallots in a saucepan. Cook over high heat until most of the liquid has reduced. Turn heat down to moderate and slowly whisk in the butter cubes. Add a few pieces at a time, whisking until all the butter is incorporated. Remove pan from heat and season with salt and pepper. Add a few splashes of balsamic vinegar if sauce needs more sharpness. Set aside.

Wash squash, trim off ends and cut into ¾" thick rounds. Scoop seeds out of each round. Place squash rounds on a lightly oiled baking sheet.

Combine oil and garlic and brush over squash. Sprinkle with salt and pepper.

Bake until just tender, about 15 minutes.

Stem shiitakes and brush with garlic, oil, salt and pepper.

Trim root hairs off scallions. Pull away outer membrane on white end of scallions. Trim away most of the scallion greens, so it is about 6" in length. Brush with garlic oil, salt and pepper.

Grill or broil the squash rounds, shiitake and scallions. Allow 6 minutes to cook vegetables, turning them after 3 minutes.

Ladle the port beurre rouge sauce onto a serving platter and arrange grilled vegetables on it.

Trade Secret: The sweetness of the port and balsamic vinegar are very pleasing and the color of the sauce is dramatic. It can be made ahead of time, as long as it is kept in a warm, but not hot place.

Serves 6
Preparation Time:
  45 Minutes
Pre-heat oven to 375°

- ¼ cup balsamic vinegar
- ¼ cup port wine
- 2 shallots, diced
- ½ lb. cold butter, cut into ½" cubes
  Salt and freshly ground black pepper
- 2 lbs. delicata squash or any edible-skin squash
- 1 lb. shiitake mushrooms
- 1 bunch scallions
- ¼ cup olive oil
- 1 garlic clove, diced fine
  Bamboo skewers for mushrooms

Annie Somerville
Greens
San Francisco, California

Vegetable Pot au Feu with Leek Vinaigrette

Serves 4
Preparation Time:
 25 Minutes
Cooking Time:
 30 Minutes

   1 qt. vegetable stock
   1 jalapeño pepper
   1 clove garlic
   2 whole cloves
   1 bay leaf
     Salt and pepper to
     taste
   2 medium carrots
   1 whole leek
   1 celery root
   4 shallots
   1 white turnip
   1 parsnip
 ½ cup red wine vinegar
 ½ cup olive oil
   1 Tbsp. Dijon mustard
   2 Tbsps. chives

 n a large stock pot, bring the vegetable stock to a boil. Add the jalapeño pepper, garlic, cloves, bay leaf, salt and pepper. Simmer for about 15 minutes. Add the whole vegetables. Cook until vegetables are tender.

Remove the vegetables from the stock and cut into thumb-size pieces, except the leek. Pass stock through a strainer and set aside.

Put the leek in a blender with the vinegar and salt and pepper to taste. Blend and pass through a fine strainer. Put the liquid back in the blender and blend in the olive oil and mustard.

Place the vegetables in a shallow soup bowl, add the broth and top with the vinaigrette. Garnish with chives.

Hitsch Albin
The Four Seasons
New York, New York

★

Steamed Vegetables in Grilled Flour Tortillas

F or the oil: Whisk olive oil, garlic, vinegar, pepper and salt together in a bowl. Place in a bottle.

For the vegetables: Toss asparagus, broccoli, zucchini, carrots, squash, scallions, mushrooms, peppers and snow peas with the oil mixture. Wrap single servings in aluminum foil, shiny side in. Bake in the oven at 350° for 10 minutes.

Serve one package of vegetables, unwrapped, with two tortillas.

Trade Secret: Serve with Mike Fennelly's Ponzu sauce, page 183.

Serves 6
Preparation Time:
  40 Minutes

  1 cup olive oil
  1 Tbsp. garlic, chopped
  ½ cup rice wine vinegar
  ½ Tbsp. black pepper, cracked
  1 Tbsp. Kosher salt
  ½ lb. asparagus, trimmed
  10 to 15 broccoli florettes
  1 zucchini, sliced lengthwise
  1 carrot, sliced lengthwise
  1 yellow squash, sliced lengthwise
  1 bunch scallions, trimmed
  15 mushrooms, wiped clean, not washed
  2 small red peppers, cut into strips
  15 snow peas, trimmed
  12 flour tortillas, lightly grilled

Mike Fennelly
Mike's on the Avenue
New Orleans, Louisiana

☆

Vegetable Tagine for Couscous

Serves 6
Preparation Time:
 30 Minutes
Cooking Time:
 1 Hour and 10 Minutes

4 Tbsps. (½ stick) butter
 or olive oil
1 onion, large, chopped
2 garlic cloves, minced
1 tsp. salt
2 tsps. paprika
½ tsp. pepper
1 tsp. ginger
2 tsps. cumin
½ tsp. cayenne pepper,
 optional
4 tomatoes, peeled,
 seeded, chopped
4 oz. chickpeas, soaked
 overnight
4 cups water or
 vegetable stock
4 carrots, peeled and cut
 into ½" lengths
2 turnips (or rutabagas)
 peeled and cut into 2"
 pieces
6 small new potatoes,
 cut into 2" pieces, or
 3 sweet potatoes, or
 peeled pumpkin, or
 butternut squash cut
 into 3" chunks
4 zucchini, cut into 2"
 lengths
½ cup raisins, plumped
 in hot water, optional
 Harissa or hot sauce to
 taste, optional

eat the butter or oil in the bottom of a large stew pot and cook the onions until tender and translucent. Add the garlic, spices and tomatoes and cook for 2 to 3 minutes longer. Add the chickpeas and 4 cups water or stock. Bring to a boil, lower the heat, cover the pan and simmer for 30 minutes. Add carrots and cook for 15 minutes, then add turnips, potatoes or sweet potatoes or pumpkin. Simmer for 10 minutes longer. Add zucchini and raisins and simmer for 15 minutes longer or until all vegetables are cooked. Adjust seasoning. Serve with couscous.

Trade Secret: Almost any combination of vegetables will work for a fragrant ragout to serve with couscous.

Joyce Goldstein
Square One Restaurant
San Francisco, California

Side Dishes

☆

Roasted Baby Artichokes

Serves 4
Preparation Time:
  30 Minutes

  2 lemons
  8 baby artichokes
    Pinch of salt
  2 garlic cloves
  ¼ tsp. kosher salt
  ⅛ tsp. cracked black
    pepper
  ½ cup fresh tomatoes,
    diced
  ⅓ cup Pinot Noir
  5 fresh thyme sprigs
  3 fresh rosemary sprigs
  8 fresh parsley stems
  2 Tbsps. balsamic
    vinegar
  3 Tbsps. olive oil
  ⅓ cup chicken stock

S queeze the juice from 1 lemon into 4 cups water. Cut the remaining lemon in half. Wash the artichokes and remove the tough or discolored outer leaves. Cut off the stem close to the base. Chop about ½″ off the top center leaves; then snip the remaining thorny tips. Squeeze lemon juice immediately on each artichoke and place them in the water mixed with lemon juice. Drain before cooking.

Place the remaining ingredients in a baking dish with the artichokes. Bake uncovered for 20 minutes at 375°. Baste occasionally with the juices from the pan. Test for doneness by piercing the bottom of an artichoke with a paring knife. If it is tender, it is done. Let cool in dish. Cut in half and remove the thistles.

Sauté until lightly brown in olive oil and serve 4 halves per person as an appetizer.

Bradley Ogden
Lark Creek Inn
Larkspur, California

Asparagus with Beurre Blanc Sauce

 ombine the wine, vinegar and shallots in a small pot. Reduce liquid over medium-high heat until only 1 tsp. remains.

Remove from heat and whisk in the butter, 1 or 2 teaspoons at a time, making sure the butter is melted before adding more. Whisk in the cream. Set sauce aside, up to 30 minutes.

Trim ends from asparagus and drop into boiling salted water. Cook for 3 minutes, strain and serve with sauce.

Serves 4
Preparation Time:
  20 Minutes

- ½ **cup dry white wine**
- ½ **cup white wine vinegar or cider vinegar**
- ¼ **cup shallots, minced**
- 1 **cup (2 sticks) unsalted sweet butter, softened**
- ¼ **cup heavy cream**
- 1 **lb. fresh asparagus**
- 1 **tsp. salt**

Chris Balcer
The Prince and The Pauper
Woodstock, Vermont

Tempura of Asparagus with Wild Mushrooms

Serves 4
Preparation Time:
  20 Minutes
(note refrigeration time)

  2 shallots, minced
  3 tsps. unsalted butter
  ½ cup wild mushrooms,
    finely chopped
    Salt and pepper to
    taste
  3 Tbsps. white wine
  ¼ cup heavy cream
  16 asparagus stalks
  1¼ cups flour
  1½ cups ice water
  1 tsp. sesame oil
  1 tsp. ginger, ground
  1 tsp. coriander, ground
  ¼ tsp. cayenne pepper
  1½ tsps. salt
  ½ cup corn starch
    Peanut oil

weat the shallots in butter. Add the mushrooms and lightly season. Deglaze with white wine and reduce until dry. Add the cream and reduce until dry. Remove from heat and cool.

Lightly score the tips of the asparagus. Quickly blanch asparagus in boiling salted water for 5 seconds, then dip in ice water. Remove from water and towel dry.

In a bowl, lightly pack the mushroom mixture around the tips of each asparagus and 2″ up the stalk. Refrigerate.

Mix the flour, ice water, sesame oil, ginger, coriander, cayenne, salt and cornstarch for the tempura batter.

Remove the asparagus from the refrigerator and lightly roll in flour, flouring only the tip of each asparagus. Dip into the tempura batter, repeating until all tips are battered. Fry tips only in peanut oil over medium heat until golden brown.

Place asparagus on the plate in a fan pattern, garnished with salad at bases.

Trade Secret: The asparagus tempura is served at the Occidental Grill on a plate of Balsamic and Black Sesame Sauce, recipe page 170.

Trent Conry
Occidental Grill
Washington, D.C.

Tangy Beets

S lice off the ends of the beets and boil until tender, about 30 minutes.

Cool, then remove skin with a small paring knife. Cut into slices, then cut each slice into match sticks.

Mix together the mustard and crème fraîche. Add to the beets and gently heat.

©"Cafe Beaujolais"

Serves 4
Preparation Time:
  10 Minutes
Cooking Time:
  30 Minutes

  8 large beets
  3 Tbsps. whole grain
    mustard with seeds
  ⅓ cup crème fraîche

Margaret Fox
Cafe Beaujolais
Mendocino, California
☆

Honey Ginger Carrots

Serves 4
Preparation Time:
 30 Minutes

- 1 lb. carrots
- 2 tsps. salt
- 4 Tbsps. butter
- ¼ cup cream
- 1 Tbsp. honey
- ¼ tsp. ginger powder
  Salt and pepper to taste

Peel carrots and cut into 2" long pieces. Place carrots in medium saucepan, cover with cold water and add salt. Bring to a boil, reduce heat and simmer for approximately 15 minutes.

Drain the carrots and place in food processor. Process to a coarse, uneven consistency.

Return carrots to saucepan over medium heat. Add butter, cream, honey and ginger, mixing well. Season with salt and pepper to taste.

Kaspar Donier
Kaspar's
Seattle, Washington

Cilantro Squash Dumplings

Combine the grilled squash, cilantro, cheese, olive oil, lime juice and zest. Season with salt and pepper. Place a small dollop of this mixture in the center of each wonton skin. Brush edges with egg and fold in half to form triangles. Press down firmly to seal.

Steam for 6 to 7 minutes until tender.

Serves 4
Preparation Time:
  20 Minutes

  1 yellow squash, grilled, diced
  2 bunches cilantro, chopped
  1 cup grated cheese, optional
  1 Tbsp. olive oil
    Juice and zest of 2 limes
    Salt and pepper to taste
 16 wonton skins
  1 egg, beaten

Peter Zimmer
Inn of the Anasazi
Santa Fe, New Mexico

Spicy Vegetable Stuffed Chiles

Serves 4
Preparation Time:
  20 Minutes
Cooking Time:
  25 Minutes

  2 Tbsps. oil
  1 medium red onion,
    thinly sliced
  2 garlic cloves, minced
  1 medium zucchini,
    ¼" diced
  1 medium chayote
    squash, peeled, pitted,
    ¼" diced
  ½ lb. tomatillos, broiled,
    blackened
  ¼ cup sour cream or
    crème fraîche
  1 cup corn kernels
  ½ tsp. salt
  2 Tbsps. fresh cilantro,
    chopped
  2 Tbsps. Italian parsley,
    chopped
    Salt to taste
  4 large Poblano chiles,
    broiled, peeled
  ⅔ cup Monterey Jack, or
    mild cheddar cheese,
    grated

 oarsely puree blackened tomatillos in a blender or food processor. Set aside.

Heat oil in a large skillet over medium heat. Add the onion and cook until beginning to brown, 7 to 8 minutes. Add the garlic and cook 2 minutes. Raise heat to medium-high and stir in the zucchini, chayote, tomatillo puree, cream, corn and salt. Stirring constantly, cook until everything is tender and the sauce is reduced to a thick coating on the vegetables, about 10 minutes. Stir in the herbs, season lightly with salt and cool while preparing the chiles.

Carefully slit the side of each chile, from the stem to the point. Carefully scrape the seeds off the seed pod and discard them. Rinse the cavity to remove stray seeds, then dry with a paper towel.

Stir the cheese into the vegetables, then use the mixture to carefully fill the cavity of each chile. Place the chiles on a greased baking dish, cover lightly with foil and bake at 350° until warm through, about 12 minutes. Serve the chiles with your favorite salsa.

Rick Bayless
Topolobampo, Frontera Grill & Zinfandel
Chicago, Illinois

Curried Eggplant

Place the eggplants in a baking pan and prick them with a fork. Bake at 450° until very tender, about 45 minutes. Drain and cool until touchable.

Peel the eggplants and transfer the pulp to a strainer. Coarsely chop the eggplant or pulse quickly in a food processor.

In a medium sauté pan over medium heat, melt the butter or warm the olive oil. Sweat the onions until translucent, about 10 minutes. Add the garlic, ginger and spices and cook for 5 minutes. Add the eggplant. Season with salt and pepper and lemon juice. Add yogurt if the eggplant flavor needs smoothing. Chopped tomatoes may be added. Garnish with chopped cilantro.

Trade Secret: This dish is rich and creamy with a little kick. If it is too hot, stir in a little yogurt to temper the spices. For those on low fat diets, steam the onions and spices in vegetable stock or water. Use non-fat yogurt and eat as much as you like!

©"Back to Square One"

Serves 6
Preparation Time:
  30 Minutes
Baking Time:
  45 Minutes

- 2 to 3 medium eggplants, 1 lb. each
- 4 to 6 Tbsps. unsalted butter or olive oil
- 2 cups chopped yellow onions
- 1 Tbsp. garlic, minced
- ¼ cup grated ginger root
- 2 tsps. coriander
- 2 tsps. ground cumin
- 1 tsp. turmeric
- ¼ tsp. cayenne, or more to taste
  Lemon juice to taste
  Yogurt, optional
- 1 cup diced tomatoes, optional
- 2 to 3 Tbsps. cilantro, chopped, optional

Joyce Goldstein
Square One Restaurant
San Francisco, California

Eggplant Scapece

Serves 4
Preparation Time:
  30 Minutes
(note marinating time)

  4 **small Japanese**
    eggplants or 1 large
    eggplant
    Oil for frying
    Salt and pepper to
    taste
  2 **cups red wine vinegar**
  1 **cup granulated sugar**
  1 **medium red onion,**
    peeled, sliced thin
  1 **Tbsp. virgin olive oil**
 10 **large mint leaves,**
    julienned

lice eggplant, with skin, on diagonal into ¼″ thick slices. Fry in oil in small batches until golden brown. Drain well on paper towels. Season with salt and pepper. Set aside.

In a sauce pot, combine the vinegar, sugar, onion and olive oil and simmer over low heat. Reserve 3 leaves of mint julienne and add the remainder to the sauce pot. Cook 20 minutes, or until onions are transparent and sauce is reduced.

In straight-sided pan, layer fried eggplant with sprinkling of mint and marinade, until it's all used. Allow to rest at least 2 hours before serving. Eggplant should be served at room temperature.

Suzette Gresham-Tognetti
Acquerello
San Francisco, California

Cheddar Cheese Grit Cakes

n a large pan, sweat the onions and garlic in butter until fragrant. Add the milk and bring to a boil while slowly stirring in grits.

Lower heat and simmer grits until tender, stirring occasionally.

Remove from heat and stir in cheese and chives. Season with salt and pepper.

Spread in ungreased pan and let cool. Cut into squares or circles and sauté quickly in butter to serve.

Serves 8
Preparation Time:
  20 Minutes

  1 **Tbsp. butter**
 ½ **white onion, diced**
  2 **garlic cloves, minced**
  3 **cups milk**
1½ **cups Haitian grits**
    (large yellow grits)
 ¾ **cup cheddar cheese,**
    grated
  2 **Tbsps. chives, chopped**
    Salt and pepper to
    taste

Hubert Des Marais
The Ocean Grand
Palm Beach, Florida

☆

Grilled Leeks with Caper Beurre Blanc

Serves 4
Preparation Time:
  30 Minutes

20 small leeks, about ½"
   in diameter
 1 cup dry white wine
 2 shallots, thinly sliced
 6 whole black
   peppercorns
 1 cup cold unsalted
   butter, cut into ½"
   pieces
 2 Tbsps. capers, coarsely
   chopped
¼ cup olive oil
   Kosher salt and freshly
   ground black pepper
 1 hard-cooked egg,
   chopped, optional
 2 Tbsps. Italian parsley,
   chopped

emove all wilted or brown outer layers from the leeks. Trim off the roots close to the end of the stalk. Do not trim too closely or the leeks will fall apart when cooked. Cut the leeks to a uniform length, 5 to 6 inches, and split the tops to within 2" of the base. Soak in cold water for 5 minutes and then rinse carefully to remove all sand and dirt. Drain.

Blanch the leeks in a large pot of boiling, salted water until the white parts are just tender when squeezed, about 5 minutes. Cool in ice-water bath, drain and set aside. The leeks can be covered and refrigerated overnight.

Place the wine, shallots and peppercorns in a small saucepan over medium heat. When the liquid has reduced to about 2 Tbsps., lower the heat and begin whisking in the butter, adding one piece at a time. Remove from heat and strain through a fine strainer. The sauce can be kept over warm (not hot) water for a few minutes while you grill the leeks. Stir in the capers, taste and add a pinch of salt if needed, just before serving.

To finish the leeks, brush them with olive oil and season with salt and pepper. Grill them until browned on both sides. Serve on a warm platter. Spoon the warm caper beurre blanc and top with egg and parsley.

Bradley Ogden
Lark Creek Inn
Larkspur, California

☆

Mozzarella al Forno

P lace the mozzarella slices in individual baking dishes. Sprinkle each baking dish with olive oil, 1 Tbsp. tomatoes, 4 olives, and ½ tsp. of basil. Bake at 450° until melted. Serve hot.

Serves 4
Preparation Time:
  10 Minutes

  4 thick slices of
    mozzarella
  2 Tbsps. olive oil
  4 Tbsps. tomatoes,
    stewed, chopped
  16 black olives, pitted
  2 tsps. basil
    Salt and pepper to
    taste

Roberto Donna
Galileo
Washington, D.C.
☆

Mushrooms and Asparagus in White Wine Sauce

Serves 4
Preparation Time:
  30 Minutes

  1 lb. fresh asparagus
  1 lb. fresh mushrooms
  4 Tbsps. butter
    Salt and pepper to
    taste
  2 Tbsps. shallots,
    chopped
  ½ cup semi-sweet white
    wine
  ½ cup cream
  ½ lb. fava beans, cooked
  2 Tbsps. chervil,
    chopped, cooked

lanch the asparagus in boiling water and slice spears diagonally.

Sauté the mushrooms in 2 Tbsps. butter and salt to taste. Add remaining butter and the chopped shallots. Deglaze with wine, reduce liquid by ⅓, then add the cream. Add the fava beans and asparagus slices.

Garnish with chopped chervil.

Gray Kunz
Lespinasse
New York, New York

Potato Pancakes

P eel and coarsely grate potatoes and onion. Place grated potatoes and onion in a large colander and squeeze to expel excess moisture. Set aside.

In a large mixing bowl beat together the eggs, salt and pepper. Mix in flour. Add the potatoes and onion and mix thoroughly.

In a large sauté pan, pour canola oil to 1" depth over medium heat. Place heaping tablespoons of potato mixture into hot oil. Cook until golden brown, turn and brown the other side. Remove from oil and drain on paper towels.

Trade Secret: Serve with apple sauce or fresh sour cream mixed with chopped scallions.

Serves 8
Preparation Time:
  15 Minutes

10 medium potatoes
1 large onion
5 eggs
  Salt and black pepper
  to taste
5 Tbsps. all-purpose
  flour
  Canola oil for frying

Kevin Johnson
The Grange Hall
Manhattan, New York

✩

Grilled New Potatoes with Garlic and Thai Chile Salsa

Serves 6
Preparation Time:
  20 Minutes

  15 to 20 small new
    potatoes, washed,
    halved vertically
1½ Tbsps. garlic, roasted,
    chopped
½ Tbsp. Serrano chile,
    finely chopped
¼ cup olive oil
¼ cup scallions, finely
    chopped
½ cup Anaheim chile,
    seeded, finely chopped
⅓ cup tomatillos or
    green tomatoes, finely
    chopped
½ Tbsp. sugar
½ tsp. Kosher salt
1½ Tbsps. lime juice
½ Tbsp. mint, finely
    chopped
1½ Tbsps. vinegar

Boil the potatoes until tender, do not overcook. Remove from water and set aside to cool.

In a mixing bowl combine the garlic, Serrano chile and olive oil. Toss with the potatoes and quickly cook on a hot grill to sear and heat through.

In a mixing bowl make the Thai Chile Salsa by combining the scallions, Anaheim chile, tomatoes, sugar, salt, lime juice, mint and vinegar.

Trade Secret: For a nice color and texture addition to the potatoes, serve with Mike Fennelly's Blackened Tomato Salsa on page 186.

Mike Fennelly
Mike's on the Avenue
New Orleans, Louisiana

Garlic Roasted Mashed Potatoes

In a medium pot, combine potatoes, water and ½ tsp. salt. Bring to a boil. Reduce to a simmer and cook until tender, about 10 minutes. Remove from heat and drain in a colander.

Return the potatoes to pot over medium heat. Add the cream, roasted garlic, white pepper and remaining salt. Mash vigorously with a potato masher until fairly smooth. Fold in butter and serve immediately.

Serves 4
Preparation Time:
20 Minutes

- 2 cups potatoes, peeled, diced to ½"
- 3 cups water
- 2 tsps. salt
- 1 cup heavy cream
- 6 garlic cloves, roasted
- ½ tsp. white pepper, ground
- 2 Tbsps. butter, unsalted

Emeril Lagasse
Emeril's
New Orleans, Louisiana

☆

String Beans with Walnuts & Lemon

Serves 4
Preparation Time:
  15 Minutes

  ½ **lb. fresh string beans**
  1 **Tbsp. butter, unsalted**
  1 **Tbsp. grated lemon**
    rind
  2 **Tbsps. walnuts,**
    coarsely chopped
    Salt and pepper to
    taste
  1 **Tbsp. lemon juice**
    Lemon wedge for
    garnish

ash and snap the ends off string beans. Blanch beans in boiling water until cooked but still firm. Drain.

In a sauté pan place butter, lemon rind and chopped walnuts. Sauté over medium heat, agitating the pan, until walnuts begin to brown. Add the warmed beans, salt and pepper, toss thoroughly and cook 1 more minute. Add the lemon juice and toss to coat beans.

Serve with a lemon wedge.

Kevin Johnson
The Grange Hall
Manhattan, New York

☆

Vegetable Ragout Tart

I n a heavy-bottomed pot, heat olive oil over medium heat. Add onion and red pepper. Let stew for 5 minutes. Raise heat slightly and add garlic, eggplant and tomatoes. Cook until liquid is absorbed. Add zucchini and thyme. Cook until zucchini is tender-crisp. Remove from heat. Add basil, salt and pepper.

Using a slotted spoon, drain off some of the oil. Divide ragout into 4 portions and mound into warm tart shells.

Serves 4
Preparation Time:
  20 Minutes

$\frac{1}{2}$ cup olive oil
1 medium onion, minced
1 large red pepper, roasted, peeled, seeded, julienned
2 garlic cloves, minced
1 small Italian eggplant, $\frac{1}{4}$" diced
4 plum tomatoes, peeled, seeded, coarsely chopped
1 medium zucchini, $\frac{1}{4}$" diced
1 sprig fresh thyme
$\frac{1}{4}$ cup fresh basil leaves, chopped
  Salt and pepper to taste
4 pre-made tart shells, or recipe page 210

Anne Rosenzweig
Arcadia
New York, New York

☆

Potato Tumbleweeds

Serves 4
Preparation Time:
  15 Minutes

  1 Tbsp. sugar
  1 Tbsp. coriander seeds
  1 Tbsp. cinnamon
  ¼ tsp. cayenne pepper
  ¼ tsp. salt
  2 cups canola oil
  1 potato, large,
    julienned
  1 sweet potato, large,
    julienned

ombine all dry ingredients and set aside.
Heat canola oil to medium heat in a saucepan. Fry the potatoes and sweet potatoes until golden and crispy. Strain oil from pan.

Dust with dry spice mix.

Trade Secret: This is an excellent accompaniment to Grilled Mushrooms on page 126 and Vegetable Pestos on pages 180, 181, and 182.

Peter Zimmer
Inn of the Anasazi
Santa Fe, New Mexico

Sauces & Condiments

Southeast Asian Sauce

Serves 6
Preparation Time:
  10 Minutes

  ½ cup lime juice
    Zest of 4 limes
  ⅓ cup light soy sauce
  ¼ cup lemon juice
  2 tsps. salt
  4 tsps. pepper
  ⅓ cup fresh ginger, finely
    chopped
  1 cup fresh basil, finely
    chopped
  8 tsps. chile oil
  8 tsps. sesame oil
1½ cups coconut milk,
    canned
  ½ cup coriander

n a mixing bowl combine all the ingredients together.

Trade Secret: Serve with your favorite oriental noodles and stir-fry dishes. Garnish this sauce with chopped roasted cashews.

Roxsand Suarez
Roxsand
Phoenix, Arizona

Avocado and Cilantro Salsa

Peel avocados and tomatoes and dice into small chunks. Mix with onions, cilantro, garlic and jalapeño peppers.

Add tomato juice, cayenne pepper, Tabasco sauce and lemon juice to taste.

Trade Secret: The avocado and cilantro salsa is a wonderful accompaniment to a chicken quesadilla.

Yield:
  1½ **Cups**
Preparation Time:
  10 Minutes

  2 **large ripe avocados**
  3 **Roma tomatoes**
  4 **Tbsps. red onions, diced**
  ½ **bunch cilantro, finely chopped**
    Garlic to taste, chopped fine
    Jalapeño peppers to taste, finely chopped
  1 **Tbsp. tomato juice**
    Cayenne pepper
    Tabasco
    Lemon juice

Joachim Splichal
Patina
Los Angeles, California

Balsamic and Black Sesame Sauce

Serves 8
Preparation Time:
  5 Minutes

  2 **cups balsamic vinegar**
  1 **garlic clove, minced**
2½ **Tbsps. black sesame**
     seeds
  1 **Tbsp. sesame oil**
     Salt and pepper to
     taste

uree all ingredients together until smooth. Serve with your favorite vegetable or fried appetizer.

Trent Conry
Occidental Grill
Washington, D.C.

Black Bean Sauce

n a food processor, pulse all the ingredients until well blended.

Trade Secret: At Roxsand, the sauce is served with the blue potato strudel, page 137. It is a wonderful accompaniment to any steamed or fresh vegetables.

Serves 4
Preparation Time:
 5 Minutes

 ½ cup light soy sauce
 4 garlic cloves
 ¼ cup fermented black
   beans, rinsed
 ¼ cup sugar
 1 chile pepper

Roxsand Suarez
Roxsand
Phoenix, Arizona

Goat Cheese Sauce

Serves 4
Preparation Time:
  15 Minutes

1½ cups white wine
  3 shallots, chopped
  ¾ cup heavy cream
  3 oz. goat cheese
  1 Tbsp. butter
    Dash of white pepper

lace white wine and shallots in a sauce pan. Reduce over medium heat to ½ liquid. Add the cream and reduce to ½ again.

Pour into a blender. Add the goat cheese and butter and blend well.

Strain and season to taste.

Thierry Rautureau
Rover's
Seattle, Washington

Park Chow-Chow

I n a mixing bowl, stir together all the chopped vegetables. Set aside until ready to cook.

In a medium saucepan, combine all the dry ingredients. Whisk in the vinegar. Bring to a boil over medium heat, stirring constantly. Add the chopped vegetables and continue cooking over medium heat, stirring regularly, about 30 minutes until sauce is thick and the vegetables are very tender. Season to taste.

Serves 8
Preparation Time:
  15 Minutes
Cooking Time:
  30 Minutes

  1 cup tomatillos or green tomatoes, finely chopped
  1 large red onion, finely diced
  1 red bell pepper, finely diced
  1 green bell pepper, finely diced
  1 yellow bell pepper, finely diced
  1 stalk celery, finely chopped
  2 cups Kosher dill pickle, finely chopped
  1 bunch scallions, finely chopped
  2 medium cucumbers, peeled, seeded, finely diced
1½ cups sugar
  ¼ cup dry mustard
  2 Tbsps. whole mustard seeds
  1 Tbsp. whole celery seeds
  ¼ cup all-purpose flour
  2 cups white vinegar
  Salt and white pepper to taste

David Beckwith
Central 159
Pacific Grove, California

☆

Gado-Gado Peanut Sauce

Serves 4
Preparation Time:
  10 Minutes

1½ tsps. sesame oil
 ⅓ cup shallots, minced
 1 garlic clove, minced
 1 tsp. fresh lemon grass,
   chopped (or ¼ tsp.
   dried lemon grass)
 1 tsp. Indonesian chile
   paste (ulek sambal)
1½ Tbsps. Indonesian soy
   sauce (ketjap manis)
1½ tsps. fresh ginger,
   grated
 ½ tsp. cumin, ground
 ½ tsp. coriander, ground
 ¼ cup peanut butter,
   unsalted
 1 cup plain yogurt, low
   fat

n a mixing bowl combine all the ingredients.

Trade Secret: This gado-gado is lightened from the typical recipe by using yogurt instead of milk. It is served at The Four Seasons with the Tofu Vegetable Roll on page 141.

Hitsch Albin
The Four Seasons
New York, New York

Caramelized Ginger Sauce

Sauté the peppers in olive oil for 3 minutes. Add brown sugar and ginger and cook 2 minutes more. Add Marsala and reduce to ⅓ liquid. Add the stock and reduce by half. Add the soy sauce, then salt and pepper to taste.

Chill until ready to serve.

Trade Secret: This sauce is a nice accompaniment to many vegetable dishes and can be prepared one day ahead.

Serves 4
Preparation Time:
20 Minutes
(note refrigeration time)

⅔ cup green and red bell peppers, finely chopped
Olive oil
¼ cup brown sugar
2 Tbsps. ginger, ground
½ cup Marsala wine
1 cup vegetable stock
2 Tbsps. soy sauce

Alex Daglis
The Place at Yesterday's
Newport, Rhode Island

Leek and Cucumber Salsa

Serves 8
Preparation Time:
  10 Minutes

  1 medium leek, washed,
    spiked (cut top to
    bottom)
  1 medium cucumber,
    peeled, seeded, cut
    into half moons
  4 medium tomatoes,
    diced
  1 serrano chile, roasted,
    skinned, seeded, finely
    diced
  1 medium red onion,
    spiked
  2 garlic cloves, finely
    chopped
  4 scallions, chopped
  ½ cup fresh cilantro,
    coarsely chopped
  ¼ cup rice wine vinegar
  ¼ cup olive oil
    Salt and pepper to
    taste

C ombine all the chopped vegetables in a large mixing bowl. Stir in the cilantro. Add the vinegar and oil and stir so that all the vegetables are evenly coated. Season to taste.

Refrigerate until ready to use. Salsa will keep 5 days when refrigerated. Serve with any vegetables, especially grilled.

David Beckwith
Central 159
Pacific Grove, California

✫

Mango and Papaya Salsa

n a mixing bowl, combine all the ingredients together. Refrigerate immediately.

Bring to room temperature before serving.

Serves 4
Preparation Time:
   15 Minutes
(note refrigeration time)

1 mango, peeled, finely
   diced
1 papaya, seeded,
   skinned, finely
   chopped
½ small tomato, seeded,
   finely chopped
1 Tbsp. red onion, finely
   chopped

Alex Daglis
The Place at Yesterday's
Newport, Rhode Island

Madeira Cream

Serves 4
Preparation Time:
  15 Minutes

  2 **Tbsps. shallots, finely**
     chopped
  ⅓ **cup Madeira**
  ¾ **cup whipping cream**

immer shallots in Madeira until liquid is reduced by half. Add cream, bring to a boil, reduce heat and simmer for 10 minutes, or to desired thickness.

Trade Secret: Serve with Susan Spicer's Goat Cheese Crouton with Mushrooms, page 30.

Susan Spicer
Bayona
New Orleans, Louisiana

☆

Flavored Oils

I n a blender, purée yellow pepper and slowly add ½ cup olive oil. Salt and pepper to taste. Set aside. Repeat the same procedure with the red pepper. Set aside.

Purée ½ cup basil in a blender while adding ½ cup olive oil.

Store all oils covered until ready to use.

Trade Secret: Flavored oils may be prepared two days ahead.

Serves 4
Preparation Time:
  20 Minutes

1½ cups olive oil
  1 yellow bell pepper, roasted, skinned, seeded
    Salt and pepper to taste
  1 red bell pepper, roasted, skinned, seeded
  ½ cup fresh basil

Alex Daglis
The Place at Yesterday's
Newport, Rhode Island

Beet Pesto

Serves 6
Preparation Time:
  5 Minutes

  1 **cup hazelnuts, roasted,**
    chopped
  2 **Tbsps. mint, chopped**
  1 **cup beet juice**
  1 **red onion, grilled,**
    finely chopped
    Juice of 1 lemon
  ½ **cup olive oil**

ombine all ingredients in a blender or food processor and purée until well combined. Season to taste with salt and pepper.

Trade Secret: This pesto is a wonderful accompaniment to fresh grilled vegetables.

Peter Zimmer
Inn of the Anasazi
Santa Fe, New Mexico

☆

Carrot Pesto

Combine all ingredients in a blender or food processor and puree until well combined. Season to taste with salt and pepper.

Trade Secret: This is an excellent accompaniment to grilled vegetables.

Serves 6
Preparation Time:
  5 Minutes

  1 cup peanuts, roasted,
     chopped
  1 Tbsp. fresh oregano,
     chopped
  1 cup carrot juice
  ½ cup olive oil
  2 chipotle chiles,
     seedless, finely
     chopped
     Juice of 2 limes

Peter Zimmer
Inn of the Anasazi
Santa Fe, New Mexico

Cilantro Pesto

Serves 6
Preparation Time:
 5 Minutes

  2 **bunches cilantro,**
   chopped
  2 **limes, juiced**
 ½ **cup pumpkin seeds,**
   roasted, chopped
 ½ **cup pine nuts, roasted,**
   chopped
 ½ **cup Parmesan cheese,**
   grated
  1 **cup olive oil**

 uree the cilantro, lime juice, pumpkin seeds, pine nuts and cheese in a blender or food processor. Add the olive oil and process until ingredients are well combined. Season to taste with salt and pepper.

Trade Secret: This pesto is a wonderful accompaniment to fresh grilled vegetables.

Peter Zimmer
Inn of the Anasazi
Santa Fe, New Mexico

Ponzu Sauce

I n a mixing bowl, combine the lemon and lime juice, rice wine vinegar, soy sauce and mirin. Let stand for 24 hours. Strain before serving.

Trade Secret: This sauce is an excellent accompaniment to vegetables. At Mike's on the Avenue, the Ponzu Sauce is served with steamed vegetables in flour tortillas, page 145.

Serves 6
Preparation Time:
  5 Minutes
(note marinating time)

- ½ cup lemon juice
- ½ cup lime juice
- ⅓ cup rice wine vinegar
- 1 cup soy sauce
- 2 Tbsps. mirin or rice wine
- 1" square Kombu (sea kelp), optional

Mike Fennelly
Mike's on the Avenue
New Orleans, Louisiana

Sabayon

Serves 4
Preparation Time:
  5 Minutes

  2 egg yolks
  2 Tbsps. white wine
  ½ tsp. fresh tarragon,
    chopped
    Salt and pepper to
    taste

ver low heat or a double boiler, whip the eggs and the wine until soft peaks form. Season with the tarragon, salt and pepper.

Trade Secret: Sabayon can be spooned over the top of any vegetable dish or casserole. On casserole-type dishes, you may want to brown it quickly under a broiler before serving.

Robert Holley
Brasserie le Coze
Coconut Grove, Florida

Tomato Coulis

Start a charcoal fire or heat the grill or broiler. Season and lightly coat the tomatoes with 2 Tbsps. olive oil. Place tomatoes on grill and cook until almost soft. Remove the seeds and strain to reserve juice. Chop the tomato pulp coarsely.

Place 2 Tbsps. of olive oil in a heavy-bottomed saucepan and heat over a moderate fire. Add the shallots and garlic and sauté for a few minutes, then add the tomato pulp and tomato juice. Blend well, then add the chiles, stock, bay leaf, wine and vinegar. Simmer for 30 minutes.

Strain coulis and discard tomato pulp and bay leaf. Place coulis back on the fire and reduce if necessary to 1½ cups. Cool coulis slightly and add the herbs. Season to taste with salt and pepper.

Trade Secret: At the Lark Creek Inn this coulis is served with a creamy wild mushroom polenta, page 99.

Yield:
  1½ Cups
Preparation Time:
  45 Minutes

    4 **large tomatoes or 1**
       28-oz. can tomatoes
    4 **Tbsps. olive oil**
  ½ **cup shallots, sliced**
    5 **garlic cloves, slivered**
    2 **serrano chiles, peeled,**
       chopped fine
  ½ **cup vegetable stock**
  ½ **bay leaf**
  ½ **cup Pinot Noir or**
       Zinfandel
  ¼ **cup balsamic vinegar**
    1 **Tbsp. basil, chopped**
    1 **Tbsp. parsley, chopped**
    1 **Tbsp. cilantro,**
       chopped
       Kosher salt to taste
       Cracked black pepper
       to taste

Bradley Ogden
Lark Creek Inn
Larkspur, California

☆

Blackened Tomato Salsa

Serves 6
Preparation Time:
  20 Minutes

  8 tomatoes
  1 red onion
1½ Tbsps. garlic, chopped
1½ Tbsps. scallions, finely
    chopped
    Juice of 1 lime
  1 Tbsp. chipotle peppers,
    finely minced, optional
  ½ tsp. Kosher salt
  ¼ tsp. white pepper
  2 Tbsps. rice vinegar
    Half of a jalapeño
    pepper, finely minced

 rill the tomatoes and onion on a grill or under a broiler until the skins are black. Do not use oil. Remove from heat and chop fine.

In a large mixing bowl combine the tomatoes and onion with the garlic, scallions, lime juice, chipotle peppers, salt and pepper, rice vinegar and jalapeño pepper.

Trade Secret: The blackened tomato salsa is served at Mike's on the Avenue with grilled new potatoes on page 162.

Mike Fennelly
Mike's on the Avenue
New Orleans, Louisiana

Roasted Tomato-Chipotle Sauce

Put the tomatoes on a baking sheet and roast 6" below a broiler until blackened, about 6 to 7 minutes. Turn and roast the other side.

Allow to cool, then peel and core tomatoes.

Put tomatoes and juice in a blender or food processor. Add chiles and make a coarse puree.

Heat the oil in a large skillet over medium heat. Add the onion and fry until beginning to brown, about 7 minutes. Add the garlic and cook 2 minutes longer. Raise the heat to medium-high. Add the tomato mixture all at once and stir constantly for a few minutes until reduced and thickened. Add the stock and let simmer until the sauce reaches a medium consistency. Add salt to taste. Remove from heat and stir in the cilantro.

Serves 6
Preparation Time:
  15 Minutes

1½ lbs. tomatoes
  2 to 3 chipotle chiles, canned
  1 Tbsp. oil
  ½ small onion, chopped
  1 large garlic clove, minced
  1 cup vegetable stock
  ½ tsp. salt
  ¼ cup cilantro, chopped

Rick Bayless
Topolobampo, Frontera Grill, and Zinfandel
Chicago, Illinois

Smoked Tomato Butter

Serves 4
Preparation Time:
  20 Minutes

  2 **medium tomatoes**
  2 **Tbsps. onion or**
    scallions, finely
    chopped
  1 **cup white wine**
  ¾ **cup (1½ sticks)**
    unsalted butter,
    softened
    Salt and pepper to
    taste

moke the tomatoes for 10 minutes in a home smoker.

Core and quarter the tomatoes. Purée in a blender.

Place the purée in a saucepan with the onions and wine and bring to a boil. Reduce heat and simmer until liquid is reduced to 1 or 2 tablespoons.

Whisk in the butter, one tablespoon at a time. The sauce should be thick and creamy. Strain, then season with salt and pepper. Serve warm but not hot.

Trade Secret: This sauce is a perfect accompaniment to serve with Susan Spicer's Vegetable Gratin with Polenta on page 124.

Susan Spicer
Bayona
New Orleans, Louisiana

Final Temptations

Mango and Kumquat Bavarian

Coconut Creme Brulée

Chocolate Decadence Cake

Polenta Pound Cake with White Chocolate Ganache

Walnut Cake

Apricot Cheesecake

Bourbon Pecan Cheesecake

Orange Ricotta Cheesecake

Raspberry Dacquoise

Caramelized Baby Eggplant

Apple Flan with Caramel Sauce

Lemon Mousse Soufflé in Blueberry Sauce

Banana Bread Pudding

Chocolate Croissant Pudding with Wild Turkey Sauce

Cranberry Bread Pudding with Warm Caramel Pecan Sauce

Apple Sorbet

Grapefruit Campari Sorbet

Raspberry Sorbet

Blood Orange Soufflé

Strawberries with Balsamic Vinegar & Red Wine

Tart Shells

Chèvre and Ginger Tart with Raspberry Sauce

Plum Almond Tart

Raspberry Almond Torte with Raspberry Sauce

Mango and Kumquat Bavarian

Serves 4
Preparation Time:
  30 Minutes
(note refrigeration time)

  5 **sheets gelatin**
  ¾ **cup mango purée**
  ¾ **cup kumquat purée**
  4 **egg yolks**
  1 **egg**
  ½ **cup sugar**
1½ **cups heavy cream**

oisten gelatin in cold water. Combine the mango and kumquat purées. Warm over a hot bain-marie, or in a dish placed in a shallow pan with warm water half-way up the dish. Add the gelatin.

Beat the eggs and sugar to a ribbon, then mix with purée. Briefly warm over a bain-marie or in pan of hot water to thoroughly dissolve gelatin. Cool.

Whip heavy cream until stiff, then fold in the purée.

Pour into a mold and refrigerate until mixture has set.

Trade Secret: Serve with a strawberry coulis.

Thierry Rautureau
Rover's
Seattle, Washington

☆

Coconut Creme Brulée

Preheat the oven to 325°.

Combine the cream, coconut milk, and 1 vanilla bean in a heavy saucepan and gradually bring to a boil. Remove the pan from heat.

In a mixing bowl, combine ¾ cup sugar and the egg yolks. Beat until smooth. Whisk the scalded cream mixture into the yolk mixture in a steady, thin stream. Strain this mixture into a separate bowl and stir in the shredded coconut.

Transfer to a round 12" baking dish. Set into a roasting pan with ½" hot water. Bake the crème brulée for about 35 minutes, or until just set. Cool to room temperature, then refrigerate until cold.

To prepare the sauce, cut the passion fruits in half widthwise and scoop out the pulp. Place the pulp in a heavy non-reactive pan. Add the vanilla bean, 1 cup sugar and water. Bring the mixture to a boil and remove the pan from the heat. Remove the vanilla bean.

Purée the raspberries with the lemon juice. Strain this mixture into the passion fruit mixture and let cool completely.

Just before serving, spoon the crème brulée mixture into the passion fruit shells. Lightly sprinkle the tops with the remaining sugar. Place under a pre-heated broiler until the sugar melts and begins to caramelize. Serve when the sugar has cooled.

Trade Secret: Spoon the sauce on the bottom of eight dessert plates. Place the crème brulées on top of the sauce and garnish with your choice of fresh fruit.

Serves 8
Preparation Time:
  1 Hour
Baking Time:
  35 Minutes

3 cups heavy cream
1 cup coconut milk, unsweetened
2 vanilla beans, split
2½ cups sugar
9 egg yolks
¾ cups shredded coconut
8 passion fruits
1 cup water
1 cup raspberries
  Juice of 1 lemon

Mark Militello
Mark's Place
North Miami, Florida

☆

Chocolate Decadence Cake

Yield:
  One 10" cake
Preparation Time:
  1 Hour, 30 Minutes
  (note refrigeration time)

1½ cups semisweet
    chocolate
½ cup unsweetened
    chocolate
1½ cups unsalted butter
1¾ cups sugar
½ cup water
7 eggs
1 cup heavy cream,
    whipped
    Extra chocolate to
    grate for garnish

ut chocolates and butter into small pieces. Put in a bowl.

Mix 1½ cups sugar with water in a saucepan and bring to a boil. Pour over chocolate and butter. Stir until melted.

Whip eggs and ¼ cup sugar in mixer until double in volume. Stir into chocolate mixture until no white streaks appear.

Pour batter into greased and paper-lined 10" cake pan. Bake at 350° on a sheet pan with 1" of water in it for about 40 to 50 minutes until it is set.

Cool cake and place in refrigerator overnight.

To release cake, dip pan in hot water and run knife carefully around the edge. Frost with whipped cream and decorate with grated chocolate.

Bradley Ogden
Lark Creek Inn
Larkspur, California

Polenta Poundcake
with White Chocolate Ganache

I n a mixing bowl combine the flour with the baking power and salt. Set aside.

In a separate bowl, combine the butter and sugar. Add the eggs one at a time, alternating with half of the flour mixture. Add the milk and vanilla, then stir in the cornmeal and sour cream. Do not overmix.

Pour into well buttered and floured loaf pans. Bake at 350° for 40 to 45 minutes until a cake tester comes out clean.

In a double boiler over hot water, slowly melt the chocolate with the liqueur. Whisk together. If too thick, add more liqueur 1 Tbsp. at a time.

Pour over the top of the cake. Cool in the refrigerator before serving.

Yield:
  2 standard loaf pans
Preparation Time:
  15 Minutes
(note refrigeration time)
Baking Time:
  45 Minutes

2¾ cups + 2 Tbsps. cake
  flour
1¼ tsp. baking powder
  ¼ tsp. salt
  ¾ cup butter (1½ sticks)
2⅔ cups powdered sugar
  3 eggs
  ¾ cup milk
1½ tsps. vanilla extract
  ⅓ cup cornmeal
  ⅓ cup sour cream
  5 oz. white chocolate,
    chopped
  ⅓ cup Creme de Cacao or
    Triple Sec

David Beckwith
Central 159
Pacific Grove, California
☆

Walnut Cake

Serves 8
Preparation Time:
  15 Minutes
Baking Time:
  35 Minutes

  1 **cup walnuts**
  ¼ **cup flour**
  ½ **tsp. salt**
  2 **tsps. baking powder**
  1 **tsp. ground cinnamon**
  ¾ **cup light brown sugar**
  5 **eggs**
  ½ **cup honey**
  ½ **cup orange juice**
  1 **tsp. vanilla extract**

utter and flour a 9″ cake pan. Put walnuts, flour, salt, baking powder and cinnamon in a food processor and blend until finely chopped. Add the brown sugar and eggs and process until smooth.

Pour the batter into the cake pan and bake at 350° for 30 to 35 minutes or until a toothpick comes out clean. Remove to a rack and cool.

Make the glaze by combining the honey, orange juice and vanilla in a saucepan, bringing the mixture to a boil.

Poke the cake with a toothpick all over before brushing generously with the glaze.

Serve in slices with fresh berries or fruit on the side.

Susan Feniger &
Mary Sue Milliken
The Border Grill
Santa Monica, California

☆

Apricot Cheesecake

L ine one 8½" springform pan with wax paper. Coat with butter. Set aside.

In a food processor, beat the cream cheese until softened, then add the sugar. Mix thoroughly, beating on medium speed. Add the apricots, then gradually add the beaten eggs to the cream cheese. Pour the mixture into the springform pan. Wrap the pan in aluminum foil to prevent leaking.

Bake at 350° for 1½ hours or until the filling has set. Refrigerate 4 hours before serving.

Trade Secret: This recipe was first created with the use of the Mamey fruit, a tropical version of the apricot. Apricots, however, are a fine substitute.

Serves 8
Preparation Time:
  30 Minutes
(note refrigeration time)
Baking Time:
  1½ Hours

  2 tsps. butter
1½ lbs. cream cheese,
    room temperature
  ¾ cup sugar
  3 apricots, peeled,
    puréed
  4 eggs, beaten

Allen Susser
Chef Allen's
Aventura, Florida

✩

Bourbon Pecan Cheesecake

Serves 12
Preparation Time:
  30 Minutes
Baking Time:
  1¾ Hours
(note refrigeration time)

2½ lbs. cream cheese
  4 eggs
  1 egg yolk
  1 cup sugar
  3 Tbsps. bourbon
  2 Tbsps. all-purpose
    flour
  2 cups graham cracker
    crumbs
  9 Tbsps. (1⅛ sticks)
    butter
¾ cup brown sugar
1½ cups pecans, chopped

arm cream cheese to room temperature. Beat the cheese, adding the 4 eggs one at a time. Add the yolk and beat until smooth. Slowly add ¾ cup sugar and bourbon. Beat until light, scraping the bottom of the bowl. Stir in the flour.

Combine the graham cracker crumbs, 3 Tbsps. melted butter and 3 Tbsps. sugar with a fork.

Press the mixture evenly into a 10″ springform cake pan.

For the topping, place the brown sugar in a small bowl. Add the remaining butter and cut until mixture resembles a coarse meal. Stir pecans into mixture.

Pour the batter into the cake pan. Bake at 325° for about 1½ hours, or until the center no longer moves when the pan is shaken. Sprinkle the topping over the cake and bake 15 minutes more. Refrigerate overnight.

Trade Secret: If you do not wish to use alcohol, substitute 1 Tbsp. lemon juice and 1 tsp. vanilla extract for the bourbon.

Chris Balcer
The Prince and The Pauper
Woodstock, Vermont

✩

Orange Ricotta Cheesecake

Beat 6 egg yolks and ½ cup sugar until well blended. Add the vanilla, ricotta, orange zest, cornmeal, cornstarch and 1 tsp. flour. Beat until smooth. Set aside.

In a separate bowl, beat 6 egg whites to soft peaks. Slowly add ¾ cup sugar, beating together until stiff.

Fold the two mixtures together and pour into a 10" pie shell. Bake at 400° for 15 minutes, then reduce heat to 350°. Continue baking for 30 minutes or until center of cake is set.

Prepare the topping in a large mixing bowl by combining the remaining flour and sugar. Add the butter and mix to a corn meal consistency.

In a separate bowl, combine the egg yolks and cream. Add the egg mixture to the flour. Do not over-beat.

Spread the topping over the cooled cheesecake.

Serves 6
Preparation Time:
  45 Minutes
Cooking Time:
  1 Hour

  7 eggs, separated
1½ cups sugar
  1 tsp. vanilla
  1 lb. ricotta cheese
     Zest of 2 oranges,
     chopped
  1 Tbsp. cornmeal
  1 tsp. cornstarch
1¼ cups + 1 tsp. flour
     Pre-cooked pie shell
  ½ cup butter (1 stick)
  2 Tbsps. cream

Celestino Drago
Drago
Santa Monica, California

☆

Raspberry Dacquoise

Serves 4
Preparation Time:
  30 Minutes
(note refrigeration time)
Baking Time:
  2½ Hours

  6 **egg whites**
  ½ **tsp. cream of tartar**
  1 **cup sugar**
  ½ **cup almonds, toasted,**
     ground
  1 **pt. raspberries**
  2 **cups heavy cream**
  ¼ **cup sugar**

race three 8″ circles on lightly greased parchment paper. Place paper circles on baking sheets.

Combine egg whites and cream of tartar in a mixing bowl. Beat until soft peaks form. Add sugar slowly while continuing to beat meringue until stiff. Fold in almonds.

Place the meringue in a pastry bag with a ½″ round tip. Squeeze out meringue onto paper circles. Smooth tops of meringue shells with a cake knife. Bake at 250° for 1 hour. Reduce oven temperature and bake for 1½ hours more. Cool for 30 minutes. Very gently remove shells from paper.

Purée raspberries and strain into a bowl. Whip cream with sugar until firm but not stiff. Fold the purée into the whipped cream.

Spread ⅓ of raspberry cream over the top of each meringue shell. Arrange a second shell on top of the cream and repeat. Place a third shell on top and decorate with remaining cream.

Chill two hours before serving.

Chris Balcer
The Prince and The Pauper
Woodstock, Vermont

✩

Caramelized Baby Eggplant

hinly slice eggplant lengthwise, leaving them attached at the tops, to be fanned out later.

Bring water to a boil. Add sugar, rum, vanilla, cinnamon and lemon. Boil until water becomes lightly syrupy.

Add eggplants and cook gently for about 10 minutes, until done but slightly firm.

Remove eggplants and continue boiling syrup until it becomes heavy. Remove from heat.

Return eggplants to syrup and cool in refrigerator.

Serve fanned out on a shallow plate with a dollop of sour cream or yogurt and a sprig of fresh mint.

Trade Secret: This sweet dish is a Basque dish with Moorish influence from Northern Spain.

Serves 6
Preparation Time:
  35 Minutes
(note refrigeration time)
Cooking Time:
  10 Minutes

  2 **lbs. Japanese**
    eggplants, small
  1 **qt. water**
  ½ **cup sugar**
  1 **Tbsp. rum**
  1 **Tbsp. vanilla extract**
  1 **cinnamon stick**
    Small pieces of lemon
    rind
  ¾ **cup sour cream or**
    yogurt
    Sprigs of fresh mint for
    garnish

Mario Leon-Iriarte
Dali
Somerville, Massachusetts

☆

Apple Flan with Caramel Sauce

Serves 6
Preparation Time:
  40 Minutes
Baking Time:
  2 Hours

  6 apples
1½ cups heavy cream
  1 cup milk
  ¾ cup sugar
  2 vanilla beans, split,
    scraped
  1 egg, beaten
  2 egg yolks, beaten
  2 cups apple juice
  ¼ cup Calvados apple
    brandy

 lice the top quarter off each apple and core, leaving a large enough hole to fill with the flan mixture. Set apples and tops aside.

In a saucepan bring 1 cup cream, milk, ¼ cup sugar and vanilla beans to a boil. Stir in the egg and egg yolks. Place over a double boiler and whisk for 10 minutes.

Place the apples in a baking dish and ladle the cream mixture into each apple. Place tops on apples and bake at 300° for 1½ to 2 hours, until done.

Prepare the caramel sauce by heating ½ cup sugar over low heat slowly until caramelized. Add the apple juice and brandy and let it reduce down to half. Add ½ cup heavy cream and cook on low heat for about 5 minutes.

To serve, place each apple on a plate and pour the sauce over the apples.

Trade Secret: Serve this dish with Chef Guenter Seeger's Apple Sorbet on the side, page 205. Ladle the sauce around it and garnish with a sprig of mint.

Guenter Seeger
The Ritz-Carlton, Buckhead
Atlanta, Georgia

✩

Lemon Mousse Soufflé with Blueberry Sauce

Prepare the soufflé by combining the yolks, sugar, lemon zest and lemon juice in a medium mixing bowl. Whisk over medium heat or over a pot of boiling water, until light and frothy.

Dissolve gelatin in water and stir gelatin into the egg mixture. Fold whipped cream into lemon mixture using soft gentle strokes.

Pour mousse into ungreased molds of your choice. Allow to set at least two hours for best results before serving.

In a heavy-bottomed saucepan, combine the blueberries, honey and brandy. Over medium heat, cook until blueberries are fully defrosted and you have a fair amount of juice in the saucepan. Reduce heat and whisk in cornstarch, stirring constantly for 2 minutes. Remove from heat and cool until ready to serve.

To serve, unmold soufflé onto individual plates. Drizzle with the blueberry sauce.

Trade Secret: The sauce and soufflé can be prepared two days in advance and will stay fresh in the refrigerator for about 4 days.

Serves 10
Preparation Time:
  20 Minutes
(note refrigeration time)

 8 **egg yolks**
 ½ **cup sugar**
   Juice and chopped zest of 3 lemons
 3 **tsps. unflavored gelatin**
 ½ **cup water**
 3 **cups cream, whipped**
 2 **bags (12 oz. each) frozen blueberries**
 2 **Tbsps. honey**
 ½ **cup brandy**
 4 **tsps. cornstarch**

David Beckwith
Central 159
Pacific Grove, California

☆

Banana Bread Pudding

Serves 4
Preparation Time:
  15 Minutes
Baking Time:
  50 Minutes

  2 **eggs or** ½ **cup egg**
     substitute
  2 **egg whites**
  1 **cup skim milk**
  4 **Tbsps. brown sugar or**
     honey
  ¼ **tsp. grated nutmeg**
  ¼ **tsp. cinnamon, ground**
  3 **slices whole-wheat**
     bread, diced
  4 **bananas, very ripe,**
     mashed
     Grated lemon rind
     (optional)

n a large bowl, whisk together the eggs and egg whites until well blended. Add the milk, sugar or honey, nutmeg and cinnamon. Add the bread and let stand for 5 minutes. Add the bananas.

Coat a 1 or 1½ qt. casserole with non-stick spray. Add the bread mixture. Place the dish in a larger baking pan and add enough hot water to come halfway up the sides of the inside pan.

Bake at 350° for 50 minutes. Remove the casserole dish from the water and allow to cool on a wire rack for 10 to 15 minutes.

Serve sprinkled with lemon rind.

Emeril Lagasse
Emeril's
New Orleans, Louisiana

☆

Chocolate Croissant Pudding with Wild Turkey Sauce

To prepare the custard, mix 10 egg yolks with ¼ cup sugar in a large mixing bowl. Add the vanilla bean and heavy cream.

In a large soup plate or individual soufflé molds, place croissant pieces and chocolate pieces together. Pour the custard over the chocolate mixture and cook in a bain marie or place molds in a larger baking pan filled with water, for 45 minutes at 200° or until firm.

Prepare the Wild Turkey sauce by bring the half & half to a boil. Remove from heat.

In a mixing bowl, beat 5 egg yolks with ½ cup sugar and add to the hot cream. Return the cream to low heat and cook until cream thickens. Add Wild Turkey to taste. Cool, then refrigerate.

Serve the chilled sauce with the pudding.

Serves 4
Preparation Time:
  15 Minutes
Cooking Time:
  45 Minutes

 15 egg yolks
 ¾ cup sugar
 1 vanilla bean, chopped
 1 qt. heavy cream
 1 croissant, toasted, cut
   into pieces
 ¼ cup chocolate,
   chopped
 1 pt. half & half
   Wild Turkey whiskey

Joachim Splichal
Patina
Los Angeles, California
☆

203

Cranberry Bread Pudding
with Warm Caramel Pecan Sauce

Serves 4
Preparation Time:
  30 Minutes
(note refrigeration time)
Baking Time:
  1 Hour

2¼ cups sugar
  1 cup water
    Zest of one orange
  1 Tbsp. vanilla extract
  2 cups cranberries
  1 lb. French bread
  5 Tbsps. butter, melted
  3 cups milk
  5 eggs
  2 tsps. cinnamon
  ½ cup brown sugar
  ½ cup heavy cream
  ¾ cup pecans, toasted,
    chopped
    Whipped cream,
    optional
    Mint sprigs for garnish

I n a sauce pan, combine 1 cup sugar, water, orange zest and vanilla. Heat to dissolve the sugar. Add the cranberries and bring the mixture to a boil. Simmer for 4 minutes. Remove from heat and cool mixture in the refrigerator for 1 hour.

Cut the French bread into 1″ chunks, drizzle with 1 Tbsp. butter and toast until golden brown. Set aside.

In a mixing bowl, whisk together the milk, ¾ cup sugar and the eggs. Stir in the toasted bread and add the chilled cranberry mixture.

Place in an oiled casserole dish and sprinkle the top with cinnamon and ½ cup sugar. Bake at 350° for one hour.

In a skillet over medium-low heat, add the remaining butter and the brown sugar. Simmer for 2 minutes while stirring. Add the pecan pieces and slowly pour in the heavy cream, while continuously whisking. Heat through.

Serve the pudding warm, drizzled with the warm caramel pecan sauce. May be garnished with whipped cream and sprigs of mint.

Alex Daglis
The Place at Yesterday's
Newport, Rhode Island

Apple Sorbet

Cut up apples into small pieces. Sprinkle juice of 1 lemon over apples and freeze until hard.

Puree frozen apple pieces in a blender with Calvados and a little syrup to taste. Strain through a fine mesh. Add more syrup or lemon juice to taste.

Process in an ice cream machine until done.

Serves 6
Preparation Time:
  10 Minutes
Freezing Time:
  2 Hours

10 apples
 2 Tbsps. Calvados
 ¾ cup syrup
 2 lemons

Guenter Seeger
The Ritz-Carlton, Buckhead
Atlanta, Georgia

Grapefruit Campari Sorbet

Serves 8
Preparation Time:
  20 Minutes
(note refrigeration time)

  3 cups sugar
  2 cups water
  ½ gal. grapefruit juice
  ¾ cup Campari

ring sugar and water to a boil in a small sauce pan. Boil 1 minute.

    Refrigerate mixture until cold. Mix with the juice and Campari.

    Freeze in an ice cream freezer or place in a bowl in the refrigerator freezer and stir every two hours until frozen, about 8 hours.

Chris Balcer
The Prince and The Pauper
Woodstock, Vermont

☆

Raspberry Sorbet

Boil the sugar and water for 12 minutes. Allow the mixture to cool. Add lemon and orange juices.
Purée the raspberries and add to the mixture. Mix in an ice cream freezer. Freeze until ready to serve.

Serves 4
Preparation Time:
 45 Minutes

2 cups sugar
2 cups water
 Juice of 1 lemon
 Juice of 1 orange
2 cups raspberries

Roberto Donna
Galileo
Washington, D.C.

Blood Orange Soufflé

Serves 6
Preparation Time:
  20 Minutes
Baking Time:
  20 Minutes

  2 **cups orange juice**
    (preferably blood
    oranges)
  2 **Tbsps. butter**
  4 **Tbsps. all-purpose**
    flour
  1 **cup whole milk**
  1 **Tbsp. orange liqueur**
  1 **vanilla bean, split**
    lengthwise
  ½ **cup sugar**
  4 **egg yolks**
    Zest of two oranges
  6 **egg whites**
  ⅛ **tsp. arrowroot or**
    cornstarch

lace orange juice in a saucepan over medium heat until reduced to ¾ cup.

In a separate stockpot, melt the butter. Add the flour and cook for 2 minutes on low heat. Add the milk and whisk in the orange liqueur. Add the vanilla bean and the sugar, reserving 1 Tbsp. of the sugar. Cook until thick and then an additional 5 minutes more. Add the orange juice. Remove from heat and cool to room temperature. Add the egg yolks and orange rind.

Whip the egg whites to soft peaks, then stir in the arrowroot or cornstarch and 1 Tbsp. sugar. Fold the whites into the soufflé.

Pour into individual soufflé dishes that have been lightly buttered and sugared. Bake for 15 to 20 minutes at 400°.

Frank McClelland
L'Espalier
Boston, Massachusetts

Strawberries with Balsamic Vinegar and Red Wine

 Rinse the strawberries and remove the stems. Cut the berries in half if they are large. Sprinkle sugar over the berries, toss and put in the refrigerator for 1 hour.

In a small bowl, combine the wine, balsamic vinegar and lemon juice. Pour over the berries and mix well before serving.

Trade Secret: Berries are delicious alone or spooned over your favorite ice cream or cheesecake.

Serves 4
Preparation Time:
   15 Minutes
(note refrigeration time)

   1 basket (pint)
      strawberries
   1 to 2 Tbsps. sugar
   1 Tbsp. red wine,
      optional
1½ tsps. balsamic vinegar
   ½ tsp. lemon juice

Suzette Gresham-Tognetti
Acquerello
San Francisco, California

✩

Tart Shells

Yield: 6 shells
Preparation Time:
  20 Minutes
(note refrigeration time)
Baking Time:
  20 Minutes

  ¾ cup + 2 Tbsps. flour
  ½ tsp. salt
  ½ tsp. sugar
  ¼ lb. sweet butter, cut
    into small pieces
  1 egg yolk
  ½ cup sour cream or
    crème fraîche

ix flour, salt and sugar. Cut butter into flour mixture until it resembles coarse cornmeal.

Mix together egg yolk and sour cream or crème fraîche and add to the flour mixture. Work together quickly until well blended and press into a ball. Wrap with plastic and refrigerate one hour.

Pat dough into six 3″ tart pans. Cover with foil and weigh down the tart shells with bags of dried beans or rice.

Chill for 15 minutes; then bake in the oven at 375° for 15 minutes. Remove weights and foil; bake another 7 minutes.

Anne Rosenzweig
Arcadia
New York, New York

☆

Chevre and Ginger Tart with Raspberry Sauce

Prepare the filling in a mixing bowl by combining the cheese with ½ cup sugar until well blended. Add 2 yolks and 1 whole egg, one at a time. Do not over-mix. Add the cream and ginger and mix until combined. Set aside.

To make the dough, use a mixer with a paddle attachment. Beat the butter and powdered sugar together until combined. Add 1 egg yolk. Do not overmix. Add the cake flour until thoroughly mixed. Let rest in the refrigerator for 30 minutes.

Roll dough out with a rolling pin. Cut to fit 4" tart pans. Place the dough in the pans and prick with a fork.

Add the filling into the tart pans and bake at 300° for about 20 minutes until set in the center and lightly brown on top. Let cool.

Prepare the sauce by puréeing the raspberries and ½ cup sugar in a blender until the sugar dissolves. Strain though a fine strainer.

To serve, spoon the sauce on a plate and top with the tart. Garnish with crystallized ginger pieces.

Serves 6
Preparation Time:
  40 Minutes
(note refrigeration time)
Baking Time:
  20 Minutes

12 oz. Chevre cheese
1 cup sugar
3 egg yolks
1 egg
1 cup cream
1 tsp. ground ginger
1 lb. butter
½ lb. powdered sugar
1½ lbs. cake flour
1 lb. frozen raspberries
  Crystallized ginger
  pieces, optional

Lisa Liggett
Mike's on the Avenue
New Orleans, Louisiana

✫

Italian Plum Almond Tart

Serves 6
Preparation Time:
  15 Minutes
Cooking Time:
  45 Minutes

  1 **cup all-purpose flour**
  ⅓ **cup + 2 Tbsps. sugar**
    Pinch of salt
  ¼ **cup almond paste**
  9 **Tbsps. butter**
  2 **egg yolks**
  1 **cup almonds, sliced**
  ½ **tsp. orange zest, grated**
    Plum liqueur or kirsch
    to taste
  2 **lbs. Italian prune**
    plums, sliced thin

repare the almond pastry shell by combining flour, 2 Tbsps. sugar, salt and almond paste in food processor bowl and pulse until blended.

Cut 6 Tbsps. cold butter into small pieces and add to mixture. Pulse again until mixture is blended. Add 1 egg yolk and pulse briefly until dough holds together when pinched.

Press dough into 9" tart pan and bake until lightly brown. Set aside and cool.

Grind almonds finely in food processor. Set aside.

Beat 1 egg yolk, ⅓ cup sugar and orange zest. Mix in 3 Tbsps. melted butter and sliced almonds. Add liqueur to taste.

Arrange plums on bottom of tart shell. Cover with almond filling, spreading with a spatula.

Bake at 350° for 40 to 45 minutes, or until filling is set.

Annie Somerville
Greens
San Francisco, California

☆

Raspberry Almond Torte with Raspberry Sauce

Mash 1 lb. of the raspberries, then place in a saucepan over medium-low heat. Cook the berries for 15 minutes, then add the syrup. Cook on low heat for 40 minutes until mixture is thick like jam. Set aside to cool.

Prepare the raspberry sauce in a saucepan by bringing 1¼ cups sugar and water to a boil for 10 minutes. While the water is boiling, purée 1¼ lbs. raspberries. Add the puréed raspberries to the sugar water. Add the Triple Sec to the sauce, cool, then refrigerate.

In a food processor prepare the cake batter by combining ¼ cup sugar and the almond paste. Add the butter, salt and vanilla and process. Add the eggs one at a time, then add the flour and baking powder.

Butter and flour a 10" springform cake pan. Pour the cake mixture into the pan and bake at 350° for 40 minutes. Do not open the oven. Turn off the oven and allow the cake to cool inside the oven for 30 minutes.

When the cake is completely cooled, cut it into two layers. Cut one layer in half again, save the other half for future use. It will freeze well. Spread the jam between the two thin layers and on top. Use remaining raspberries to cover the entire top. Drizzle with the raspberry sauce.

Trade Secret: A beautiful presentation is to slice one piece of cake and place in the middle of a dish with sauce on one side and a scoop of raspberry ice cream on the other side.

Serves 6
Preparation time:
  1 Hour
Baking Time:
  1¼ Hours

3¾ lbs. raspberries
2 cups simple syrup
1½ cups sugar
½ cup water
½ cup Triple Sec
1 cup almond paste
1¼ cups butter, room
  temperature
⅛ tsp. salt
1 Tbsp. vanilla extract
6 eggs
2 cups flour
½ Tbsp. baking powder.

Roberto Donna
Galileo
Washington, D.C.

Here are the finest chefs in America. They offer tips, advice, criticism and trade secrets. This is what they have to say.

Listen
to the
Chefs

Great cooks must have a passion for food and eating. They must taste all the time, both in their heads and in their mouths. Cooks at home should cook what they love, then eat what they cook. My cooking is special because I believe in big flavors in honest, rustic Italian-inspired food. The four basic elements — salt, sugar, acid and fat — are balanced. When I look at a recipe, I look for fun combinations of flavors and techniques.

On summer vacation when I was 12, I spent the summer at a hotel helping the chef. From then on, I was hooked on cooking. When I look at a recipe, I look for fresh ingredients with an innovative approach. Tips for the cook at home: change the menu; experiment; try a variety of things. A good quick meal: pasta. What makes a great cook? To be in love with food and to have good taste. When I dine out, I look for unusual food with a different twist.

Economics got me interested in cooking. I enjoyed cooking as a child. My first full-time job after college was as a short-order cook. Then I went on to the Culinary Institute in New York. When I dine out, I prefer northern Italian, Oriental, traditional regional Italian and regional American. A tip for home cooks: Go out to eat! Keep your cooking as simple as possible. Read the recipe through, then make sure all the ingredients are on hand. A good, quick meal: pizza. Three ingredients I can't live without: tomatoes, garlic and olive oil.

I look for depth in recipes, meaning that the person who developed it knows something about combining and developing flavors. When I dine out, I prefer ethnic cooking where care is put into food with traditional flavors. Many cooks at home try to cook too quickly, thus cutting out the elements that give the dish deep, rich flavor. A good, quick meal: omelette, salad and some good bread. Three ingredients I can't live without: anything in the onion family, chiles, acidic flavors such as citrus and vinegar. I use only really good, fresh ingredients and treat them with great respect.

Other restaurants: Frontera Grill, Zinfandel

A great cook must have patience and a keen sense of curiosity about food. He or she must enjoy problem-solving. A good pair of comfortable shoes also helps. Be patient and organized. Pay attention to detail and read new recipes twice before attempting them. This will save you time and will give you a complete understanding of methods and techniques needed for the recipe. When I dine out, I prefer almost any type of ethnic food, as long as it's well prepared. There is so much honesty and tradition there — I find that very refreshing.

My grandmother whetted my culinary interests when I was just 3 years old. When I dine out, I prefer Chinese, which I have not learned to cook on purpose, so I *must* dine out. Many cooks go wrong because they memorize recipes; learn *how* to cook, not just specific recipes. My advise to home cooks: have fun and keep trying. What makes a great cook? A great palate and an inborn instinct.

Born in Brooklyn and trained in France, my New American cuisine takes the best native ingredients in season, uses my training, then pushes the culinary boundaries a little. My French training always influences my food, but I'm starting to dabble in Afro-American food. Other influences, such as Asian flavors, are also finding their way into my menus. I like to think I offer a glimpse into the 21st century, if I may be so bold. I encourage young African-Americans to look into the field of cooking. The jobs are there and the money is good if you're willing to work hard.

A great cook is somebody who truly enjoys cooking, works hard and enjoys making people happy. Cooks at home should be organized and should have all the ingredients prepared before starting a recipe. Cook the vegetables crisp and use a meat thermometer when cooking all meat and poultry. A good quick meal: pasta, tossed in good olive oil, garlic, fresh tomato, basil and anything left over in the fridge. I like to put five or six flavors on each plate.

A great cook is someone who has a love of food. Don't be discouraged if something doesn't work out the first time — keep on trying. When I dine out, I look for ethnic foods and foods that I don't prepare everyday. My recommendation for a good quick meal: a seafood stew or a simple pasta dish. I can't live without wine, onions, bread, fresh herbs, produce and fresh seafood.

My parents owned a grocery store next to a small restaurant. That was my playground. In order to keep me out of his way, the chef taught me to cook. Love for the heart of cooking is what makes a great cook. Many cooks go wrong because they think compli-cated recipes are the best. That is not true. A good, quick meal: a bowl of pasta. A good tip for cooks at home: keep it simple.

I grew up on a farm in northern Sicily. My family grew, raised and made almost everything we ate — pressing the olives for oil, making fresh mozzarella from the milk of our cows, and raising pigs for sausage and prosciutto. At the age of 15, I left home to train in a restaurant in Pisa. Three ingredients I can't live without: olive oil, Parmesan cheese and tomatoes.

Other restaurant: Il Pastaio

I don't like hoity-toity places that make food look good, but it doesn't have any backbone. I like food with soul, food with guts. I'm never surprised when things go wrong in the kitchen. If I've learned one thing in my life, it's to be patient. At my restaurant, we don't use recipes. If you don't have the feeling in your hands and the taste in your mouth — those are the tools of a good chef. I'm most often associated with Southwestern food, but when I eat out, I like pizza, barbecue, Chinese or Mexican food. Always use solid classical techniques and ingredients indigenous to your area.

A great cook is someone who loves to eat, is experimental, good with their hands, sensitive — and smart. When I dine out, I like Indian and Asian food the most; for lunch, Middle Eastern and Ethiopian are more and more of interest. Good tips for cooks at home: taste constantly while cooking, then stop and think about the food and adjust the taste. Also, use hot pans when sautéing. A good quick meal: feta, avocado, olive oil, bread and steamed artichoke. I like bold, strong flavors and appreciate the down-home or street food — the true kitchen of each country at its best.

Other restaurant: City Restaurant

I got interested in cooking because I found it to be an artistic collaboration, plus it offered immediate gratifying results. Many professional cooks cut corners on ingredients and steps in a recipe. I would advise the home cook to use cookbooks as a guideline, then do your own thing. A good quick meal: quesadillas with goat cheese, sun-dried tomatoes and shiitake mushrooms. Three ingredients I can't live without: ginger, chiles and tomatoes.

A great cook is someone with an excellent palate, a curiosity about foods, a willingness to experiment and make mistakes — then make them right. I look for three things in a recipe: complexity of flavors and textures, ease of preparation, and not-too-exotic ingredients. A good, quick meal: Polenta with sausages and steamed greens. Three ingredients I can't live without: garlic, onions and chocolate — not all together, though. I care about putting out the best possible food, whether homey or fancy.

What do I look for in a recipe? Clarity of organization, a point of view about flavor. Many home cooks don't plan ahead or have quality ingredients to begin with. They make poor substitutions and then wonder why the dish didn't come out. The three ingredients I can't live without: garlic, lemon and olive oil. And remember, don't try to do too much at one time. I try to understand the history behind the dish and how the flavors come together.

A great cook needs a good palate, a repertoire of culinary skills and no fear of venturing away from what the recipe says. Conceptualize instead of gluing yourself to a recipe. Follow it, learn the idea, then deviate. Many home cooks don't trust their instincts when it comes to taste. Be comfortable and confident to try what you know tastes good. People have been eating for thousands of years. It's very difficult to create something entirely new. I enjoy revitalizing and renovating old classics and personalizing them with my own interpretation.

I became interested in cooking because I always enjoyed helping my mother when I was a child. When I consider a recipe, I look for the availability of ingredients, the ease of preparation and the time involved. I like many kinds of food when I dine out. A great cook is someone who truly enjoys cooking. Three ingredients I can't live without: olive oil, butter and herbs. What makes my cooking special is the blend of French with the Southwestern.

I got interested in cooking through watching and helping my mother in the kitchen. Also, it's a lot easier making an omelette than painting the fence. I prefer recipes that provide taste with as little preparation and conflicting ingredients as possible. Cooks at home should use common sense: think before you start your recipe. Sometimes I, too, have trouble in my kitchen at home, trying to prepare too many difficult dishes in a certain period of time. Keep your recipes simple. Remember that food is alive — cook it properly and use lots of love.

My mother and grandmother were great cooks. I started cooking at age 7 for the family. When I see a recipe, I look for simplicity — to be true to a region is to be true to the dish. Many cooks at home don't taste along the way. Be true to your own palate. A good quick meal: a bowl of polenta and a Caesar salad. Three ingredients I can't live without: olive oil, thyme and garlic. What makes my cooking special is attention to detail and tasting all the time as I go along. I seek harmony of balance, texture and taste.

My grandfather and grandmother were my chief inspirations to cook. My mother, though, taught me how to bake when I was about 8 or 9. I look for recipes that are simple, direct and easy to interpret. The taste of the end product should reveal the essential ingredients, not mask them. When I dine out, I prefer Vietnamese food. Great cooks have creativity, imagination and an intuitive sense of how food works together. Don't be afraid to try new and exotic ingredients — you never know what you might learn.

Cooking is love. When you cook, you romance the food. If I am in a bad mood, I usually don't cook. Many cooks go wrong when they compromise the flavor for looks. Cooks are not landscape designers or florists — our dishes should taste good. Three ingredients I can't live without: olive oil, bread and garlic. I never went to cooking school; I was a doctor. I cook as if I'm going to eat it — you always want the best for yourself. When I dine out, I look for simple foods, particularly Italian and Middle Eastern.

The creative aspect is what got me interested in cooking. Plus, both of my brothers are chefs. Here's what makes a great chef: lots of hard work, a passion for food, being a team leader, seeking perfection. Home cooks should stick to simplicity. Try to spend a day or two in a professional kitchen to learn some handy tricks. Many cooks lack good fundamentals in classic cuisine, therefore they miss the essential item proposed, or they mix and match incorrectly. Being born in the Far East but classically trained, I love using spices in combination with the best seasonal products available, including Asian flavors.

My passion for cooking began in my New England youth with a Portuguese mother and French-Canadian father. I'd come home from school and say to my mother, "Let's cook." Later, I turned down a music scholarship so I could pursue my first love — cooking — at a culinary school. When I came to New Orleans, the people, the culture, the spice and the hospitality all felt like home. There is a tremendous melting pot of flavors from the Cajuns, Creoles, French and Spanish.

Other restaurant: Nola

Cooks at home should have all their ingredients ready before they start to cook. Many cooks go wrong because they handle the food too much during the cooking process — or they overcook it. Three ingredients I can't live without: garlic, olive oil and, of course, wine. My cooking is special because I insist on a strong fidelity to the original recipes, then I add touches of today's world.

When I look at a recipe, I imagine how it is going to taste. I don't look for easy recipes; I always look for something interesting, then alter the recipe to my own liking. A great cook must have originality, a sense of style and a good palate. Home cooks should not be afraid of baking or trying new recipes. Many home cooks go wrong when they over-mix ingredients. A good, quick meal: Chinese stir-fry. I like to do individual desserts and pastries. I use a lot of fruit and color as garnishes. I like desserts to be three-dimensional, not flat. When I dine out, I like Indian food.

My grandmother got me interested in cooking. A great cook has good tastebuds, pays attention to detail, artistic presentation and commitment to the customer. Cooks at home should not be afraid to experiment with new ingredients and seasonings. Many cooks go wrong because they don't taste their food. A good quick meal: vegetable quinoa with wild mushrooms. Three ingredients I can't live without: wild mushrooms, organic lettuces and fresh herbs. When I dine out, I prefer ethnic foods.

My love of cooking began while cooking with my grandparents. My grandmother was a strong German chef. I still keep her cookbooks for emotional support. I no longer use recipes; I try to get inspired by the ingredients or combinations of ingredients. Home kitchens should be stocked with standard appliances that make cooking easier. Home cooks should prep as much ahead as possible. Grilling is a great way to cut down on cooking time. Many cooks at home go wrong because they put too much on a plate. They need to step aside to see what they are doing.

When I was 14, my father began designing and building restaurants for two friends; consequently, it was easy for me to get a summer job. That's how I got interested in cooking. When I see a recipe, I look for an idea that I can develop or take to another level. Many cooks go wrong because they don't taste their food enough in order to adjust seasoning. Cooks at home should read the recipe from beginning to end, then think about how they can improve it.

My mother's passion for delicious and interesting food got me interested in cooking. Plus the enjoyment I get from working with my hands. I look for balanced flavors that make sense in a recipe. A great cook tastes often and imagines the experience of eating a whole dish of whatever she's tasting. Good tip for home cooks: follow your own tastes when adjusting a recipe. A good quick meal: shredded chicken salad. Three ingredients I can't live without: onions, pepper, olive oil — and, of course, salt.

Other restaurant: City Restaurant

The greatest influence on my cooking came from my early exposure to fresh, native American foods. Coming from the Midwest, I grew up with freshly caught trout, free-range chickens, and hand-picked fruits and vegetables. Good tips: keep it simple; use the freshest ingredients available and put them together in such a way that the flavors, colors and textures combine to bring out the best in each other.

Other restaurant: One Market Restaurant

When I look at recipes, I look for a perfect match of ingredients. When I dine out, I look for food that demonstrates the passionate cook behind it. A great cook has feeling, passion, a willingness to be consistent. Many cooks go wrong because they do not use the basics of cooking in the right order. Three ingredients I can't live without: extra virgin olive oil, fresh herbs and all my homemade vinegars.

I was an anthropologist in Africa and learned people's culture by having them teach me to cook. That's how I became interested in cooking. I look for simplicity in a recipe. A tip for cooks at home: use the best ingredients; one can cook very simply and plainly and still have a wonderful meal. Many cooks go wrong by over-complicating things. Three ingredients I can't live without: kale, parsley and butter.

I learned the importance of fresh, quality ingredients when I grew up in Germany surrounded by my parents' produce business. When I dine out, I look for food that is prepared with care from the freshest ingredients. Many cooks mix too many things together — that leads to conflicting seasoning and flavors. My cooking is special because I try to capture the moment of creativity; I strive for spontaneous cuisine.

Cooking meals for the community Zen center and vegetarian food got me interested in cooking. When I dine out, I prefer Asian food. A great cook is one who has a great sense of taste, sensitivity to what's in season and a willingness to work with what's there. Some good tips for cooks at home: use fresh ingredients, grow or buy good produce, try a planter box with fresh herbs. A good quick meal: pasta, potatoes, polenta. What makes my cooking special is that I pay attention to all steps in a planning order. I put a tremendous amount of care into the finished product.

I got interested in cooking because my mom is a good cook and I have always been interested in eating. When I dine out, I gravitate toward ethnic foods — either Thai, Mexican or Vietnamese. Cooks at home should follow a recipe once, then personalize it later. Three ingredients I can't live without: citrus, olive oil and cheese. A good, quick meal: bake a potato, then be creative. I have a good feel for combining ingredients and creating interesting food combinations. I use my good taste as a filter for different styles of cuisine.

I got interested in cooking because my parents had a small inn in the Black Forest. When I dine out, I look for good food, whether it is Italian, Japanese, Chinese or French. Good tip for cooks at home: buy the best seasonal ingredients and you're halfway there. A good quick meal: pasta with tomato and basil. Three ingredients I can't live without: potatoes, olive oil and tomatoes.

Other restaurant: Pinot Bistro

I got interested in cooking because I love seeing the bounty of fresh ingredients arranged on a work table. A great cook should have a good eye, nose and palate. Home cooks should plan their menus while at the market. Don't rush the initial cooking time of base ingredients which support the rest of the recipe. A good, quick meal: pasta and stir-fried vegetables. Three ingredients I can't live without: onions, garlic and ginger. When I dine out, I look for Mexican food cooked by simple, country-type cooks.

I began to cook because I was inspired by my grandmother's love of cooking and how it brought the family together. When I dine out, I look for clean, well-prepared dishes that are not overly fussy — very often I tend toward Japanese. Too many cooks are scared to get their hands dirty; they try to simplify the cooking preparation too much. Cooks at home should be flexible. Try to understand what an ingredient's purpose is so you can adjust a recipe to your taste.

I was inspired to become a cook while traveling through France at the age of 19. When I look at a recipe, I look for inspiration from the main ingredients, not at the exact proportions or techniques. When I dine out, I prefer Indian food. A great cook must be close to the garden, must understand the ingredients. Good tip: shop first, get the ingredients, then decide on a recipe. Shop at the farmers' market and buy what is in season. A good quick meal: grilled chicken on a bed of lettuces with lemon vinaigrette.

How did I get interested in cooking? I come from a big Italian family, so I spent a lot of time in the kitchen when I was little. A great cook must have creativity and artistic ability. Food comes from your imagination — that is how you develop your flavors, textures and colors. Many cooks go wrong because they over-season and over-flavor things when they should start simply and let the food speak for itself. A good quick meal: grilled fish with some greens and a vinaigrette. What makes my cooking so special? It comes from the heart. When I dine out, I prefer Italian; I love pasta.

I wanted to be a musician and was a semi-pro at one time. Then I found cooking to be as creative and satisfying. It involves the same senses and emotions — plus taste. Cooks at home should pretend there are no rules; they should use their emotions. Many cooks look at textbooks too much. They follow the rules instead of feeling the food. A good quick meal; wok-seared kale with roasted garlic and balsamic vinegar.

"With years a richer life begins,
The spirit mellows:
Ripe age gives tone to violins,
Wine and good fellows."

– John Townsend
Trowbridge
1827 – 1916

Wine Pairings

F ine wines go well with all types of food. It's all in knowing how flavors — both subtle and strong — can be enhanced for fuller enjoyment.

Until recently, strictly vegetarian tables were noticeably deficient in wines.But now we know that wine, used in moderation, reduces stress, aids in digestion, and most certainly enriches the palate of the discriminating diner.

Here is a guide to help you pair good wines with the exquisite flavors of our recipes. Whenever possible, we suggest particular wines for particular dishes in this book. The important thing is to match the various flavors to your own palate. Then **you** decide, based on what you like.

White Wines

CHARDONNAY — This premiere white wine, often very dry, is rich, buttery and full. The grapes, grown mostly in California and France, result in a very popular wine that is sometimes spicy or nutty, with a hint of the wood from the barrels in which it is aged. The Chardonnays aged in French oak are described as having hints of vanilla, butterscotch, cloves or peaches. Excellent with delicate dishes because the flavors don't compete and overpower one another.

SAUVIGNON BLANC — Full-bodied wine with a grassy, herbaceous flavor and a distinctively fruity bouquet. One variation, Fume Blanc, a name derived in California, stresses a rich, smoky flavor. Many good French vintages are available as well. Try Sauvignon Blanc with the jalapeño corn flan or the sweet potato bisque.

CHENIN BLANC — This is a fruitier, slightly sweeter wine than either Chardonnay or Sauvignon Blanc. Its grassy flavor is an excellent enhancement to any of the risottos or light pasta dishes.

PINOT BLANC — While you will find this wine to be crisp and dry, it does not display the full flavors and intensity of either Chardonnay or Sauvingon Blanc. But its grassy character will go well with intense foods. Try it with the goat cheese crouton with mushrooms or the Vidalia onion tart.

GEWÜRZTRAMINER — Let's start with pronunciation: Ge-WURZ-tra-mee-ner. Noted for its fruity, spicy flavor, it often tends to sweetness. Good varieties come from Germany, France and California. You can find Gewürztraminer in varying degrees of sweetness. The drier versions go well with hot, spicy dishes; the sweeter late-harvest versions go well on their own as dessert wines.

RIESLING — Originally from Germany, Riesling (pronounced REEZ-ling) is very adaptable because it can be either sweet or dry. Generally, it has a delicate, flowery bouquet and spicy, fruity flavor. Try a Riesling with most non-spicy vegetarian dishes. You will find it goes well with the garden paella or the grilled portobello mushroom club.

Red Wines

CABERNET SAUVIGNON — Perhaps the most popular of the red wines, this full-bodied wine — whether from France's Bordeaux region or from several of California's vintage regions — is rich and complex. It goes well with meats, so it tends to overpower many vegetarian dishes. Try it with tomato-based pastas or grilled dishes.

MERLOT — This wine tends to be softer and mellower than Cabernet, while similar in flavor. Lush and full-flavored, it is often blended with Cabernet grapes in order to cut its tannic bite. It can be earthy and smoky, exhibiting hints of cherry and mint. Try it with the vegetable lasagna or the blue potato strudel.

PINOT NOIR — This delicate yet rich wine — originally from France's Burgundy region but now well-produced in several American regions — is becoming more and more popular. Its complex and subtle nature makes it very compatible with many vegetarian dishes. Pair it with the hearty wild mushroom risotto or a vegetable ragout.

ZINFANDEL — Here is a red wine for all tastes. Typically fruity, varieties range from light and soft to complex and full-bodied. You will detect some spicy, raspberry flavors in the wine. Some varieties are robust enough to challenge Cabernet Sauvignons. It should be particularly good with full, hearty dishes such as raviolis, risottos and ragouts.

Champagne

In the United States, the term Champagne is used to describe most sparkling wine. More correctly, true Champagne comes only from France's Champagne district. In any event, the celebrated bubbly wine is a wonderful accompaniment to many vegetarian dishes. It also comes in a wide variety, from dry to sweet. Try it at brunch or as an aperitif as well. We recommend it with the sweet garlic Capri cheese souffle or the onion on potatoes with truffle vinaigrette.

Dessert Wines

You will find a large variety of sweet wines, sometimes fortified with brandy, appropriate for dessert. Some of the more popular dessert wines include Sauterne, Sherry, Madeira, Late Harvest Riesling, Port and some sparkling wines, such as Spumante. Your best bet is to sample several sweet wines, then decide which suits your palate best. We recommend a dessert wine with the apple flan with caramel, apricot cheesecake, and the chevre and ginger tart.

Conversion Index

LIQUID MEASURES

1 dash	3 to 6 drops
1 teaspoon (tsp.)	1/3 tablespoon
1 tablespoon (Tbsp.)	3 teaspoons
1 tablespoon	1/2 fluid ounce
1 fluid ounce	2 tablespoons
1 cup	1/2 pint
1 cup	16 tablespoons
1 cup	8 fluid ounces
1 pint	2 cups
1 pint	16 fluid ounces

DRY MEASURES

1 pinch	less than 1/8 teaspoon
1 teaspoon	1/3 tablespoon
1 tablespoon	3 teaspoons
1/4 cup	4 tablespoons
1/3 cup	5 tablespoons plus 1 teaspoon
1/2 cup	8 tablespoons
2/3 cup	10 tablespoons plus 2 teaspoons
3/4 cup	12 tablespoons
1 cup	16 tablespoons

VEGETABLES AND FRUITS

Apple (1 medium)	1 cup chopped
Avocado (1 medium)	1 cup mashed
Broccoli (1 stalk)	2 cups florets
Cabbage (1 large)	10 cups, chopped
Carrot (1 medium)	1/2 cup, diced
Celery (3 stalks)	1 cup, diced
Eggplant (1 medium)	4 cups, cubed
Lemon (1 medium)	2 tablespoons juice
Onion (1 medium)	1 cup diced
Orange (1 medium)	1/2 cup juice
Parsley (1 bunch)	3 cups, chopped
Spinach (fresh), 12 cups, loosely packed	1 cup cooked
Tomato (1 medium)	3/4 cup, diced
Zucchini (1 medium)	2 cups, diced

APPROXIMATE EQUIVALENTS

1 stick butter = ½ cup = 8 Tbsps. = 4 oz.
1 cup all-purpose flour = 5 oz.
1 cup cornmeal (polenta) = 4½ oz.
1 cup sugar = 8 oz.
1 cup powdered sugar = 4½ oz.
1 cup brown sugar = 6 oz.
1 large egg = 2 oz. = ¼ cup = 4 Tbsps.
1 egg yolk = 1 Tbsp. + 1 tsp.
1 egg white = 2 Tbsps. + 2 tsps.

Metric Conversions

OUNCES TO GRAMS

To convert ounces to grams, multiply number of ounces by 28.35

1 oz...........30 g.	6 oz.........180 g.	11 oz. ......300 g.	16 oz. ......450 g.
2 oz...........60 g.	7 oz.........200 g.	12 oz. ......340 g.	20 oz. ......570 g.
3 oz...........85 g.	8 oz.........225 g.	13 oz. ......370 g.	24 oz. ......680 g.
4 oz. ....115 g.	9 oz.........250 g.	14 oz. ......400 g.	28 oz. ......790 g.
5 oz. ....140 g.	10 oz. ......285 g.	15 oz. ......425 g.	32 oz. ......900 g.

QUARTS TO LITERS

To convert quarts to liters, multiply number of quarts by 0.95

1 qt..............1 L	2½ qt........2½ L	5 qt. ....4¾ L	8 qt...........7½ L
1½ qt. ......1½ L	3 qt. ....2¾ L	6 qt...........5½ L	9 qt...........8½ L
2 qt..............2 L	4 qt. ....3¾ L	7 qt...........6½ L	10 qt.........9½ L

FAHRENHEIT TO CELSIUS

To convert Fahrenheit to Celsius, subtract 32 from the Fahrenheit figure, multiply by 5, then divide by 9

OTHER METRIC CONVERSIONS

To convert **ounces to milliliters,** multiply number of ounces by 30

To convert **cups to liters,** multiply number of cups by 0.24

To convert **inches to centimeters,** multiply number of inches by 2.54

Mail Order Sources

If you are unable to locate some of the specialty food products used in *The Great Vegetarian Cookbook*, you can order them from the mail order sources listed below. These items are delivered by UPS, fully insured and at reasonable shipping costs.

CHEESE

Crowley Cheese
Healdsville Road
Healdsville, VT 05758
(802) 259-2340
Smoked, mild, medium and sharp cheeses, plus spiced cheeses such as garlic, sage and hot pepper.

Ideal Cheese
1205 Second Ave.
New York, NY 10021
(212) 688-7579
Imported Italian cheeses.

Mozzarella Company
2944 Elm St.
Dallas, TX 75226
(800) 798-2654
(214) 741-4072
(214) 741-4076 fax
Goat cheese, mascarpone, mozzarella, pecorino, ricotta and other cheeses.

Tillamook County Creamery Association
P.O. Box 313
Tillamook, OR 97141
(503) 842-4481
(800) 542-7290
Over 30 types of cheeses, black wax cheese, and a hot jalapeño cheese.

CHOCOLATES AND CANDY

The Brigittine Monks Gourmet Confections
23300 Walker Lane
Amity, OR 97101
(503) 835-8080
(503) 835-9662 fax
Popular items are chocolate with nuts and pecan pralines.

Festive Foods
9420 Arroyo Lane
Colorado Springs, CO 80908
(719) 495-2339
Spices and herbs, teas, oils, vinegars, chocolate and baking ingredients.

COFFEE AND TEA

Brown & Jenkins Trading Co.
P.O. Box 2306
South Burlington, VT
   05407-2306
(802)862-2395
(800) 456-JAVA
Water-decaffeinated coffees featuring over 30 blends such as Brown & Jenkins Special blend, Vermont Breakfast blend and Hawaiian Kona, in addition to 15 different flavors of teas.

Stash Tea Co.
P.O. Box 90
Portland, OR 97207
(503) 684-7944
(800) 826-4218
Earl Grey, herbal teas like peppermint, ruby mint, orange spice and licorice flavors.

DRIED BEANS AND PEAS

Baer's Best
154 Green Street
Reading, MA 01867
(617) 944-8719
Bulk or 1-pound packages of over 30 different varieties of beans, common to exotic. No peas.

Corti Brothers
5801 Folsom Blvd.
Sacramento, CA 95819
(916) 736-3800
Special gourmet items such as: imported extra-virgin olive oils, wines, exotic beans, egg pasta.

Dean & Deluca
560 Broadway
New York, NY 10012
(800) 221-7714
(212) 431-1691
Dried beans, salted capers, polenta, arborio rice, dried mushrooms, dried tomatoes, parmesan and reggiano cheeses, kitchen and baking equipment.

DRIED MUSHROOMS

Dean & Deluca
560 Broadway
New York, NY 10012
(800) 221-7714
(212) 431-1691
Dried beans, salted capers, polenta, arborio rice, dried mushrooms, dried tomatoes, parmesan and reggiano cheeses, kitchen and baking equipment.

G.B. Ratto & Co.
821 Washington St.
Oakland, CA 94607
(800) 325-3483
(510) 836-2250 fax
Imported pasta, dried beans, amaretti cookies, semolina flour, dried mushrooms, dried tomatoes, parmesan and reggiano cheeses.

Gold Mine Natural Food Co.
1947 30th St.
San Diego, CA 92102-1105
(800) 475-3663
Organic foods, dried foods, whole grain rice, Asian dried mushrooms, condiments, sweeteners, spices.

FLOURS AND GRAINS

Dean & Deluca
560 Broadway
New York, NY 10012
(800) 221-7714
(212) 431-1691
Dried beans, salted capers, polenta, arborio rice, dried mushrooms, dried tomatoes, parmesan and reggiano cheeses, kitchen and baking equipment.

G.B. Ratto & Co.
821 Washington Street
Oakland, CA 94607
(510) 832-6503
(800) 325-3483
Flours, rice, bulgar wheat, couscous, oils, and sun-dried tomatoes.

Gold Mine Natural Food Co.
1947 30th St.
San Diego, CA 92102-1105
(800) 475-3663
Organic foods, dried foods, whole grain rice, Asian dried mushrooms, condiments, sweeteners, spices.

King Arthur Flour Baker's Catalogue
P.O. Box 876
Norwich, VT 05055
(800) 827-6836
Semolina flour, all types of flours, wheat berries, kitchen and baking equipment.

The Vermont Country Store
P.O. Box 3000
Manchester Center, VT 05255-3000
(802) 362-2400 credit card orders
(802) 362-4647 customer service
Orders are taken 24 hours a day.
Many different varieties: whole wheat, sweet-cracked, stone-ground rye, buckwheat, cornmeal and many more. They also sell a variety of items which are made in Vermont.

FRUIT & VEGETABLES

Diamond Organics
Freedom, CA 95019
(800) 922-2396
Free catalog available.
Fresh, organically grown fruits & vegetables, specialty greens, roots, sprouts, exotic fruits, citrus, wheat grass.

Giant Artichoke
11241 Merritt St.
Castroville, CA 95012
(408) 633-2778
Fresh baby artichokes.

Lee Anderson's Covalda Date Company
51-392 Harrison Street (Old Highway 86)
P.O. Box 908
Coachella, CA 92236-0908
(619) 398-3441
Organic dates, raw date sugar and other date products. Also dried fruits, nuts and seeds.

Northwest Select
14724 184th St. NE
Arlington, WA 98223
(800) 852-7132
(206) 435-8577
Fresh baby artichokes.

Timber Crest Farms
4791 Dry Creek Road
Healdburg, CA 95448
(707) 433-8251
Domestic dried tomatoes and other unsulfured dried fruits and nuts.

HONEY

Howard's Happy Honeybees
4828 Morro Drive
Bakersfield, CA 93307
(805) 366-4962
Unfiltered flavored honeys, such as orange blossom and sage honeys in addition to honey candy.

KITCHEN AND BAKING EQUIPMENT

A Cook's Wares
211 37th St.
Beaver Falls, PA 15010-2103
(412) 846-9490

Dean & Deluca
560 Broadway
New York, NY 10012
(800) 221-7714
(212) 431-1691
Dried beans, salted capers, polenta, arborio rice, dried mushrooms, dried tomatoes, parmesan and reggiano cheeses, kitchen and baking equipment.

La Cuisine
323 Cameron St.
Alexandria, VA 22314
(800) 521-1176

The Chef's Catalog
3215 Commercial Ave.
Northbrook, IL 60062-1900
(800) 338-3232
(708) 480-8929

Williams-Sonoma
Mail Order Dept.
P.O. Box 7456
San Francisco, CA 94120-7456
(800) 541-2233 credit card orders

(800) 541-1262 customer service
Vinegars, oils, foods and kitchenware.

NUTS

Gourmet Nut Center
1430 Railroad Avenue
Orland, CA 95963
(916) 865-5511
Almonds, pistachios and cashews.

Koinonia Partners
1324 Hwy 49 South
Americus, GA 31709
(912) 924-0391
Shelled/unshelled, flavored pecans and peanuts in addition to chocolates and different varieties of fruitcakes.

PASTA

Corti Brothers
5801 Folsom Blvd.
Sacramento, CA 95819
(916) 736-3800
Special gourmet items such as: imported extra-virgin olive oils, wines, exotic beans, egg pasta.

G.B. Ratto & Co.
821 Washington St.
Oakland, CA 94607
(800) 325-3483
(510) 836-2250 fax
Imported pasta, dried beans, amaretti cookies, semolina flour, dried mushrooms, dried tomatoes, parmesan and reggiano cheeses.

Morisi's Pasta
John Morisi & Sons, Inc.
647 Fifth Avenue
Brooklyn, NY 11215
(718) 499-0146

(800) 253-6044
Over 250 varieties available from this 50-year old, family-owned gourmet pasta business.

PASTRY AND BAKED GOODS

Cafe Beaujolais Bakery
P.O. Box 730
Mendocino, CA 95460
(707) 937-0443
Panfortes, almond and hazelnut pastries as well as fruit cakes, jam, chocolate and home-made cashew granola.

SAFFRON

Vanilla Saffron Imports, Inc.
949 Valencia Street
San Francisco, CA 94110
(415) 648-8990
(415) 648-2240 fax
Saffron, vanilla beans and pure vanilla extract, dried mushrooms as well as herbs.

SEEDS FOR GROWING HERBS AND VEGETABLES

Herb Gathering, Inc.
5742 Kenwood Ave.
Kansas City, MO 64110
(816) 523-2653
Seeds for growing herbs, fresh-cut herbs.

Shepherd's Garden Seeds
6116 Highway 9
Felton, CA 95018
(408) 335-6910
Excellent selection of vegetable and herb seeds with growing instructions.

The Cook's Garden
P.O. Box 535
Londonderry, VT 05148
(802) 824-3400
*Organically grown, reasonably
priced vegetable, herb and flower
seeds. Illustrated catalog has growing tips and recipes.*

Vermont Bean Seed Company
Garden Lane
Fair Haven VT 05743
(802) 273-3400
*Selling over 60 different varieties of
beans, peas, corn, tomato and flower
seeds.*

W. Atlee Burpee & Co.
Warminster, PA 18974
(800) 888-1447
*Well-known, reliable, full-color seed
catalog.*

Well-Sweep Herb Farm
317 Mount Bethal Rd.
Port Murray, NJ 07865
(908) 852-5390
*Seeds for growing herbs, fresh herb
plants.*

SPECIALTY FOODS AND FOOD GIFTS

China Moon Catalogue
639 Post St.
San Francisco, CA 94109
(415) 771-MOON (6666)
(415) 775-1409 fax
*Chinese oils, peppers, teas, salts,
beans, candied ginger, kitchen sup-
plies, cookbooks.*

Corti Brothers
5801 Folsom Blvd.
Sacramento, CA 95819
(916) 736-3800
*Special gourmet items such as:
imported extra-virgin olive oils,
wines, exotic beans, egg pasta.*

Festive Foods
9420 Arroyo Lane
Colorado Springs, CO 80908
(719) 495-2339
*Spices and herbs, teas, oils, vinegars,
chocolate and baking ingredients.*

G.B. Ratto & Co.
821 Washington St.
Oakland, CA 94607
(800) 325-3483
(510) 836-2250 fax
*Imported pasta, dried beans,
amaretti cookies, semolina flour,
dried mushrooms, dried tomatoes,
parmesan and reggiano cheeses.*

Gazin's Inc.
P.O. Box 19221
New Orleans, LA 70179
(504) 482-0302
*Specializing in Cajun, Creole and
New Orleans foods.*

Gold Mine Natural Food Co.
1947 30th St.
San Diego, CA 92102-1105
(800) 475-3663
*Organic foods, dried foods, whole
grain rice, Asian dried mushrooms,
condiments, sweeteners, spices.*

Knott's Berry Farm
8039 Beach Boulevard
Buena Park, CA 90620
(800) 877-6887
(714) 827-1776

*Eleven types of jams and preserves,
nine of which are non-sugar.*

Kozlowski Farms
5566 Gravenstein Highway
Forestville, CA 95436
(707) 887-1587
(800) 473-2767
*Jams, jellies, barbecue and steak
sauces, conserves, honeys, salsas,
chutneys and mustards. Some products are non-sugared, others are in
the organic line. You can customize
your order from 65 different products.*

Williams-Sonoma
Mail Order Dept.
P.O. Box 7456
San Francisco, CA 94120-7456
(800) 541-2233 credit card
   orders
(800) 541-1262 customer
   service
*Vinegars, oils, foods and kitchen-
ware.*

SPICES AND HERBS

**Apple Pie Farm, Inc. (The
Herb Patch)**
Union Hill Rd. #5
Malvern, PA 19355
(215)933-4215
A wide variety of fresh-cut herbs.

Festive Foods
9420 Arroyo Lane
Colorado Springs, CO 80908
(719) 495-2339
*Spices and herbs, teas, oils, vinegars,
chocolate and baking ingredients.*

Fox Hill Farm
444 West Michigan Avenue
P.O.Box 9
Parma, MI 49269
(517) 531-3179
Fresh-cut herb plants, topiaries,
ornamental and medicinal herbs.

Meadowbrook Herb Gardens
Route 138
Wyoming, RI 02898
(401) 539-7603
Organically grown herb seasonings,
high quality spice and teas.

Nichols Garden Nursery
1190 N. Pacific Hwy
Albany, OR 97321
(503) 928-9280
Fresh herb plants.

Old Southwest Trading
Company
P.O.Box 7545
Albuquerque, NM 87194
(800) 748-2861
(505) 831-5144
Specializes in chiles, everything from
dried chiles to canned chiles and
other chile-related products.

Penzey Spice House Limited
P.O. Box 1633
Milwaukee, WI 53201
(414) 768-8799
Fresh ground spices (saffron, cinna-
mon and peppers), bulk spices, seeds,
and seasoning mixes.

Rafal Spice Company
2521 Russell Street
Detroit, MI 48207
(800) 228-4276
(313) 259-6373
Seasoning mixtures, herbs, spices,
oil, coffee beans and teas.

Spice Merchant
P.O. Box 524
Jackson Hole, WY 83001
(307) 733-7811
Specializes in Asian spices.

VERMONT MAPLE SYRUP

Butternut Mountain Farm
P.O.Box 381
Johnson, VT 05656
(802) 635-7483
(800) 828-2376
Different grades of maple syrup, also
a variety of honey and fruit syrups
such as raspberry and blueberry.

Green Mountain Sugar House
R.F.D. #1
Ludlow, VT 05149
(802) 228-7151
(800) 647-7006
Different grades of maple syrup,
maple cream and maple candies, in
addition to cheese, fudge and
creamed honey.

VINEGARS AND OILS

Community Kitchens
P.O. Box 2311, Dept. J-D
Baton Rouge, LA 70821-2311
(800) 535-9901
Vinegars and oil, in addition to
meats, crawfish, coffees and teas.

Corti Brothers
5801 Folsom Blvd.
Sacramento, CA 95819
(916) 736-3800
Special gourmet items such as:
imported extra-virgin olive oils,
wines, exotic beans, egg pasta.

Festive Foods
9420 Arroyo Lane
Colorado Springs, CO 80908
(719) 495-2339
Spices and herbs, teas, oils, vinegars,
chocolate and baking ingredients.

Kermit Lynch Wine Merchant
1605 San Pablo Ave.
Berkeley, CA 94702-1317
(510) 524-1524
(510) 528-7026 fax

Kimberly Wine Vinegar
Works
290 Pierce Street
Daly City, CA 94015
(415) 755-0306
Fine wine vinegars and northern
California olive oil.

Select Origins
Box N
Southampton, NY 11968
(516) 288-1382
(800) 822-2092
Oils, vinegars and rice.

Williams-Sonoma
Mail Order Dept.
P.O. Box 7456
San Francisco, CA 94120-7456
(800) 541-2233 credit card
   orders
(800) 541-1262 customer
   service
Vinegars, oils, foods and kitchen-
ware.

Glossary of Ingredients

ACHIOTE: a spice blend made from ground annatto seeds, garlic, cumin, vinegar and other spices.

ACORN SQUASH: an oval-shaped winter squash with a ribbed, dark-green skin and orange flesh.

ANAHEIM CHILE: elongated and cone-shaped chiles that are red or green with a mild flavor.

ANCHO CHILE: a shiny-skinned red or green cone-shaped chile with medium heat.

ARBORIO RICE: a large-grained plump rice which requires more cooking time than other rice varieties. Arborio is traditionally used for risotto because its increased starches lend this classic dish its creamy texture.

ARMENIAN CUCUMBER: a long, pale, green-ridged cucumber with an edible skin, also known as the English cucumber.

ARUGULA: also known as rocket or roquette, noted for its strong peppery taste. Arugula makes a lively addition to salads, soups and sautéed vegetable dishes. It's a rich source of iron as well as vitamins A and C.

ASIAN NOODLES: though some Asian-style noodles are wheat-based, many others are made from ingredients such as potato flour, rice flour, buckwheat flour and yam or soybean starch.

BALSAMIC VINEGAR: made from the juice of Trebbiano grapes and traditionally aged in barrels, this tart, sweet, rich vinegar is a versatile ingredient.

BARTLETT PEAR: this large, sweet, bell-shaped fruit has a smooth, yellow-green skin that is sometimes blushed with red.

BASMATI RICE: translated as "queen of fragrance," basmati is a long-grained rice with a nut-like flavor and fine texture.

BÉCHAMEL SAUCE: a basic French white sauce made by stirring milk into a butter-flour roux. Béchamel, the base of many other sauces, was named after its inventor, Louis XIV's steward Louis de Béchamel.

BELGIAN ENDIVE: a white, yellow-edged bitter lettuce that is crunchy.

BLOOD ORANGE: a sweet-tart, thin-skinned orange with a bright red flesh.

BOK CHOY: resembles Swiss chard with its long, thick-stemmed, light green stalks. The flavor is much like cabbage.

BOUQUET GARNI: a group of herbs, such as parsley, thyme and bay leaf, that are placed in a cheesecloth bag and tied together for the use of flavor in soups, stews and broths.

BULGAR WHEAT: wheat kernels that have been steamed, dried and crushed, offering a chewy texture.

CAPERS: available in the gourmet food sections of supermarkets, capers are a small, green, pickled bud of a Mediterranean flowering plant; usually packed in brine.

CARDAMOM: a sweetly pungent, aromatic cooking spice that is a member of the ginger family.

CHANTERELLE MUSHROOM: a trumpet-shaped mushroom that resembles an umbrella turned inside out. One of the more delicious wild mushrooms.

CHÉVRE: cheese made from goat's milk is lower in fat and offers a delicate, light and slightly earthy flavor.

CHICKPEAS: also called garbanzo beans, they have a firm texture and mild, nut-like flavor. Available canned, dried or fresh.

CHICORY or **CURLY ENDIVE:** a crisp, curly, green-leafed lettuce. Best when young. Tend to bitter with age.

CHILE OIL: a red oil available in Asian stores. Chile oil is also easily made at home by heating 1 cup of vegetable or peanut oil with 2 dozen small dried red chiles or 1 Tbsp. cayenne.

CHIPOTLE PEPPERS: ripened and smoky-flavored jalapeño peppers have a fiery heat and delicious flavor.

CHOW-CHOW: a mustard-flavored mixed vegetable and pickle relish.

CLARIFIED BUTTER: also called drawn butter. This is an unsalted butter that has been slowly melted, thereby evaporating most of the water and separating the milk solids, which sink to the bottom of the pan. After any foam is skimmed off the top, the clear butter is poured off the milk residue and used in cooking.

COCONUT MILK: available in Asian markets, this milk is noted for its richly flavored, slightly sweet taste. Coconut milk can be made by placing 2 cups of finely grated chopped fresh coconut in 3 cups scalded milk. Stir and let stand until the milk cools to room temperature. Strain before using.

COULIS: a general term referring to a thick purée or sauce.

COURT BOUILLON: a broth made by cooking various vegetables and herbs in water.

CRÈME FRAÎCHE: a bit richer than sour cream, yet more tart than whipped heavy cream. It can be purchased in most supermarkets or made by whisking together ½ cup heavy or whipping cream, not ultra-pasteurized, with ½ cup sour cream. Pour the mixture into a jar, cover and let stand in a warm, dark area for 24 hours. This will yield 1 cup which can be kept in the refrigerator for about 10 days.

CRESS: resembles radish leaves, with a hot peppery flavor.

EGGPLANT: commonly thought of as a vegetable, eggplant is actually a fruit. The very narrow, straight Japanese or Oriental eggplant has a tender, slightly sweet flesh. The Italian or baby eggplant looks like a miniature version of the common large variety, but has a more delicate skin and flesh. The egg-shaped white eggplant makes the name of this fruit understandable.

FAVA BEANS: tan flat beans that resemble very large lima beans. Fava beans can be purchased dried, canned or fresh.

FLOWERS, EDIBLE: can be stored tightly wrapped in the refrigerator, up to a week. Some of the more popular edible flowers are the peppery-flavored nasturtiums, and chive blossoms, which taste like a mild, sweet onion. Pansies and violas offer a flavor of grapes. Some of the larger flowers such as squash blossoms can be stuffed and deep-fried.

FRISÉE: sweetest of the chicory family, with a mildly bitter taste. The leaves are a pale green, slender but curly.

FROMAGE BLANC CHEESE: fresh, day-old curds with some of the whey whipped back into the cheese. The texture is similar to ricotta cheese and is available plain or flavored.

GADO-GADO: this Indonesian favorite consists of a mixture of raw and slightly cooked vegetables served with a spicy peanut sauce.

GANACHE: a rich chocolate icing made of semisweet chocolate and whipping cream that are heated and stirred together until the chocolate has melted.

GNOCCHI: the Italian word for "dumplings," gnocchi are shaped into little balls, cooked in boiling water and served with butter and Parmesan or a savory sauce. The dough can also be chilled, sliced and either baked or fried.

GORGONZOLA CHEESE: a blue-veined Italian creamy cheese.

GRAHAM FLOUR: whole-wheat flour that is slightly coarser than the regular grind.

GRITS: coarsely ground grain such as corn, oats or rice. Grits can be cooked with water or milk by boiling or baking.

HABANERO CHILE: tiny, fat, neon orange-colored chiles that are hotter than the jalapeño chile.

HAZELNUT OIL: a lightly textured oil with a rich essence of hazelnut.

HUMMUS: this thick Middle Eastern sauce is made from mashed chickpeas seasoned with lemon juice, garlic and olive oil or sesame oil.

JALAPEÑO CHILE: these plump, thumb-size green chiles are known for wonderful flavor.

JICAMA: grows underground like a tuber, yet is part of the legume family. Beneath the thick brown skin, the flesh is creamy-white and sweet. Tastes like a cross between an apple and a potato.

KALAMATA OLIVES: intensely flavored, almond-shaped, dark purple Greek olives packed in brine.

KOSHER SALT: an additive-free, coarse-grained salt that is milder than sea salt.

LEMON GRASS: available in Asian food stores, this citrus-flavored herb has long, thin, gray-green leaves and a scallion-like base. Available fresh or dried.

LENTILS: the French or European lentil is grayish-brown with a creamy flavor. The reddish-orange Egyptian or red lentil is smaller and rounder. Lentils should be stored airtight at room temperature and will keep about 6 months. Lentils offer calcium and vitamins A and B, and are a good source of iron and phosphorus.

MÂCHE: also known as lamb's lettuce, has a delicate, sweet-nutty taste. The lettuce is a deep green.

MANGO: grows in a wide variety of shapes: oblong, kidney and round. Its thin, tough skin is green and, as the fruit ripens, becomes yellow with red mottling. Under-ripe fruit can be placed in a paper bag at room temperature.

MARJORAM: there are many species of this ancient herb, which is a member of the mint family. The most widely available is sweet marjoram or wild marjoram. Early Greeks wove marjoram into funeral wreaths and planted it on graves to symbolize their loved one's happiness, both in life and beyond.

MARSALA: a wine with a rich, smoky flavor that can range from sweet to dry.

MESCLUN: a traditional French mixture of tiny lettuces, including curly endive, red lettuce, Romaine, oak-leaf, butter lettuce and rocket.

MIRIN: a sweet cooking sake.

MISO: a fermented salty soybean paste made by crushing boiled soybeans with barley.

MOREL MUSHROOM: a wild mushroom that is cone-shaped with a spongy beige cap. Has a nutty taste.

NAPA CABBAGE: also known as Chinese cabbage, it looks like a cross between celery and lettuce, very much like romaine lettuce. The flavor is more delicate with a slight peppery taste.

NASTURTIUM FLOWERS: edible sweet and peppery flowers in a rainbow of colors. Nasturtiums are beautiful in salads and easy to grow.

NORI: paper-thin sheets of dried seaweed ranging in color from dark green to dark purple to black. Nori is rich in protein, vitamins, calcium, iron and other minerals.

OPAL BASIL: a beautiful purple basil with a pungent flavor.

OREGANO: this herb belongs to the mint family and is related to both marjoram and thyme, offering a strong, pungent flavor. Greek for "joy of the mountain," oregano was almost unheard of in the U.S. until soldiers came back from Italian World War II assignments raving about it.

OYSTER MUSHROOM: a beige fan-shaped wild mushroom with a mild flavor and soft texture.

PARMESAN CHEESE: a hard dry cheese made from skimmed or partially-skimmed cow's milk.

PECORINO CHEESE: a cheese made from sheep's milk

POLENTA: cornmeal — ground corn kernels, white or yellow, often enriched with butter and grated cheese. A staple of northern Italian cooking.

PORCINI MUSHROOM: The parasol-shaped mushroom cap has a thick stem, with a meaty, smoky flavor.

QUINOA: served like rice or as a base for salads. Pale yellow in color and slightly larger than a mustard seed with a sweet flavor and soft texture.

RADICCHIO: this peppery-tasting lettuce with brilliant, ruby-colored leaves is available year-round, with a peak season from mid-winter to early spring. Choose heads that have crisp, full-colored leaves with no sign of browning. Store in a plastic bag in the refrigerator for up to a week.

RICE WINE VINEGAR: a light, clean-tasting vinegar that works perfectly as is, in salads, as well as in a variety of Asian-inspired dishes.

RISOTTO: an Italian rice specialty made by stirring hot stock in Arborio rice that has been sautéed in butter.

ROMAINE: known for a sweet nutty flavor, this lettuce has long, crisp, green or red leaves.

ROUX: a mixture of melted butter or oil and flour used to thicken sauces, soups and stews. Sprinkle flour into the melted, bubbling-hot butter, whisking constantly over low heat, cooking at least 2 minutes.

SAFFRON: a bright yellow, strongly aromatic spice that imparts a unique flavor. Store saffron in a cool dark place for up to 6 months.

SAVOY CABBAGE: also known as curly cabbage, has lacy leaves with a white or reddish trim.

SERRANO CHILE: a fat, squat, red or green hot chile. They are milder when roasted with the ribs and seeds removed.

SHIITAKE MUSHROOM: a Japanese mushroom sold fresh or dried, which imparts a distinctively rich flavor to any dish. The versatile shiitake is suitable for almost any cooking method including sautéing, broiling and baking.

SNOW PEAS: a translucent, bright green pod that is thin, crisp and entirely edible. The tiny seeds inside are tender and sweet. Snow peas are also called Chinese snow peas and sugar peas.

SORBET: a palate refresher between courses or as a dessert, the sorbet never contains milk and often has softer consistency than sherbet.

SOY MILK: higher in protein than cow's milk, this milky, iron-rich liquid is a non-dairy product made by pressing ground, cooked soybeans. Cholesterol-free and low in calcium, fat and sodium, it makes an excellent milk substitute.

SPAGHETTI SQUASH: a yellow watermelon-shaped squash whose flesh, when cooked, separates into spaghetti-like strands.

STRUDEL: a type of pastry made up of many layers of very thin dough spread with a filling, then rolled and baked until crisp.

SUN-DRIED TOMATOES: air-dried tomatoes sold in various forms such as marinated tomato halves, which are packed in olive oil, or a tapenade, which is puréed dried tomatoes in olive oil with garlic.

TAHINI: Middle Eastern in origin, tahini is made from crushed sesame seeds. Used mainly for its creamy, rich and nutty flavor as well as for binding food together.

TEMPEH: made from cultured, fermented soybeans; comes in flat, light, grainy-looking cakes.

TOFU: a versatile fresh soybean curd, tofu is an excellent and inexpensive form of protein. It is characteristically bland in taste, but can be enhanced with seasonings.

TOMATILLOS: green husk tomatoes; small with a tart, citrus-like flavor .

TRUFFLE: a fungus that grows underground near the roots of trees prized by gourmets for centuries. Truffles should be used as soon as possible after purchase, but can be stored up to 6 days in the refrigerator or for several months in the freezer. Canned truffles, truffle paste and frozen truffles can be found in specialty stores.

VIDALIA ONION: the namesake of Vidalia, Georgia where they thrive. This yellow onion, sweet and juicy, is available in the summer or by mail- order year-round.

WATERCRESS: this spicy-flavored green is dark in color with glossy leaves.

Recipe Index

About the Author

 KATHLEEN DEVANNA FISH, author of the popular "Secrets" series, is a gourmet cook who is always on the lookout for recipes with style and character.

In addition to *The Great Vegetarian Cookbook*, the California native has written *The Great California Cookbook, California Wine Country Cooking Secrets, San Francisco's Cooking Secrets, Monterey's Cooking Secrets, New England's Cooking Secrets, Cape Cod's Cooking Secrets* and *Cooking and Traveling Inn Style*.

Before embarking on a writing and publishing career, she owned and operated three businesses in the travel and hospitality industry.

She and her husband, Robert, live on a boat in the Monterey harbor with their black lab, Dreamer.

 ROBERT FISH, award-winning photojournalist, produces the images that bring together the concept of the "Secrets" series.

In addition to taking the cover photographs, Robert explores the food and wine of each region, helping to develop the overview upon which each book is based.

Bon Vivant Press

P.O. Box 1994
Monterey, CA 93942
800-524-6826
408-373-0592
408-373-3568 FAX

Send _____ copies of *The Great Vegetarian Cookbook* at $14.95 each.

Send _____ copies of *The Great California Cookbook* at $14.95 each.

Send _____ copies of *California Wine Country Cooking Secrets* at $13.95 each.

Send _____ copies of *San Francisco's Cooking Secrets* at $13.95 each.

Send _____ copies of *Monterey's Cooking Secrets* at $13.95 each.

Send _____ copies of *New England's Cooking Secrets* at $14.95 each.

Send _____ copies of *Cape Cod's Cooking Secrets* at $14.95 each.

Add $3.00 postage and handling for the first book ordered and $1.50 for each additional book. Please add $1.08 sales tax per book, for those books shipped to California addresses.

Please charge my ☐ Visa
☐ MasterCard # _____

Expiration date_____Signature _____

Enclosed is my check for _____

Name_____

Address _____

City_____State_____Zip _____

☐ This is a gift. Send directly to:

Name_____

Address _____

City_____State_____Zip _____

☐ Autographed by the author
   Autographed to _____